THE NEW COMPLETE BULLDOG

The New Complete
BULLDOG

by Colonel Bailey C. Hanes

FOURTH EDITION
Third Printing—1983

HOWELL BOOK HOUSE Inc.
230 Park Avenue, New York, N.Y. 10169

Library of Congress Cataloging in Publication Data
Hanes, Bailey C
   The new complete bulldog, by Bailey C. Hanes. 3d ed.
New York, Howell Book House, 1973.

   First published in 1956 under title: The complete
bulldog.

1. Bulldogs.   I. Title.
SF429.B85H3   1973   636.7'2   73–78984
ISBN 0–87605–066–6   MARC
ISBN 0–87605–068–2
Library of Congress   73 [4]

To My Son,
Dr. Bailey Frank Hanes

Ch. Bronco's Linebacker Two, owned by Mr. and Mrs. G. H. Mosley, has brought in many fine wins during his show career. One of the highest-ranking Bulldogs in the United States during the late 1970s, he was #2 in 1978 and #1 in 1979 with three BIS, 12 G1s and 20 other placings.

Contents

Preface

I WOULD like to take this opportunity to thank everyone who had a part in producing this book. I want especially to extend my appreciation to Mr. H. S. Hodson of Bournemouth, England, without whose help the compiling of the history of the Bulldog would have been a near-impossibility. He also gave me a great deal of assistance in securing many of the old prints and paintings that appear as illustrations.

I extend my gratitude to Mr. and Mrs. Raymond L. Dickens, Mr. Don Moon, Dr. and Mrs. Malcom E. Phelps, and Mrs. Louise Rucks for their aid, counsel, and timely suggestions. And my heartfelt thanks to all of the Bulldog fanciers who so kindly supplied me with photographs of their dogs. Last but not least, the writing of this book could never have been accomplished without the untiring help and encouragement of my wife.

I first felt a need for a book of this kind a number of years ago when I began to breed and show Bulldogs and could not find the breed information I needed. In 1948 I began to collect the information contained in this book. I believe the reader will find all the information to be factual, as I have not only been very careful in recording the facts and events, but as a double check, when that part of the manuscript pertaining to the early history of the breed was completed, I sent it to Mr. H. S. Hodson, the greatest living historian on the breed, and he kindly consented to check it for authenticity and accuracy.

It has now been 25 years since the first edition of THE COMPLETE BULLDOG came off the press and was so favorably received by the public. For some time Howell Book House and I have felt the need for a new edition. This revised edition is the result of that need and the research and recording of events of the past ten years. New text and photographs have been added to update the first edition.

In writing this book it has been my hope that each and every reader, whether or not he may breed Bulldogs, will gain something worthwhile. If I have accomplished my purpose I will feel repaid for the undertaking, which I assure you, was much greater than I had anticipated.

Col. Bailey C. Hanes

Foreword

I FOUND out later that the day I read Bailey C. Hanes' manuscript for *The Complete Bulldog*, the temperature reached 107 degrees. I'm one who complains bitterly and hates the heat in any degree, and my family came home that night expecting to find me in a state of collapse. Their faces were a collective study when I said no, I hadn't been especially warm. I had been reading a book. A dog book? Yes, but a book that is considerably more than just a book about dogs.

Hanes' history and study of a breed is also a study of a people. From the time you reach the "Nothing exceeded the fury with which the Bulldog fell upon other animals . . ." you are like a Bulldog about this book. You can't, or won't let go. Your eyes leap from one paragraph to the next. When you have finished you feel better about people. You feel that the English-speaking part of the world has come a long, long way. That, at least, it has learned compassion.

Bailey Hanes is a quiet, unassuming man, soft spoken. He takes his time and does things right. And the amazing part is that he gets so many things done—youth work, church work, the projects of the Lions Club in his town of Guthrie. His work with dogs began when

11

he was a boy. Since 1948 he has owned Bulldogs—good ones. He has an American Kennel Club judging license and is past president of the Oklahoma City Kennel Club, the oldest all-breed club in the State.

The Complete Bulldog began in 1948 as a hobby of collecting data, old prints, old out-of-print books on Bulldogs, in-print books which had anything to do with the breed. Most of the material for the history came from England. Hanes painstakingly checked with English authorities on every shred of information before it went into his book as fact.

Some time ago I ran a column on making kennel dogs a means to an end, rather than an end in themselves. To illustrate my point, I used an old painting (Bulldogs and an English background) which belongs to Bailey Hanes, who imported the painting from England, and I told a little about his book. It wasn't surprising that Bulldog breeders were interested, or that other breeders were. But here's what happened that was surprising: since that time I have answered as many questions about the book as I have about dogs. People who don't own dogs, as well as those who do, want to read *The Complete Bulldog* and have requested that they be informed the minute the book comes out.

May the same labor of love that Bailey Hanes has taken on for Bulldogs be taken on someday by others for other breeds.

LOUISE RUCKS
Former President
Dog Writers' Association of America

12

Historical Background
of the Bulldog

As a beginning, let us make a very brief study of the known history of the dog down through the ages. Paleontologists inform us that they are able to trace the ancestry of the dog for about fifty-five million years. Originally, the present dog and the bear may have had a common ancestor. It is generally agreed that dogs have followed four general trends of evolutionary development. First, there were the gigantic bear-dogs, possibly the direct ancestors of the bears, dogs in which size was at a premium. Second, there were the hyena-like dogs, common only to North America and constituting a type which eventually became extinct. Finally, there were the two branches of dogs as we know them today: in the one group, the hunting dogs of India and Africa, very much like the wolves, but with a separate family history; and in the other group, the wolves, wild dogs, and foxes, which may be considered as a central stem in the tree of our domesticated dogs.

In the Holy Bible we find fourteen references to dogs, the first appearing in Genesis and indicating that dog and man may have been companions from the beginning of man's existence.

It is generally supposed that the Phoenician traders brought the fierce Mollossian dogs of the ancient Greeks to England in the sixth century B. C., and that here the Mastiff type fixed itself. It is believed by some that this early Mastiff dog was the foundation of our modern Bulldog.

In the very early history of the dogs of England, we are told that the ancient Britons took into battle with them large, ferocious, and formidable dogs. Early writers have indicated that the Gauls purchased Bulldogs for use in war and used them in battle, along with their native dogs, to combat the enemy. Many historians believe that both the English Mastiff and the modern Bulldog are descendants of these war dogs of faraway times.

The ancestry of the Bulldog, or rather his claim to originality, has long been a subject of controversy among naturalists. Buffon considers the Bulldog as the parent of the Mastiff, while Sydenham Edwards contends that the Bulldog resulted from an intermixture of the large Mastiff and the Pug dog—not the Pug dog of France, but the Pug which is also known as the small or Dutch Mastiff, and which originated in Holland and Germany.

It is now generally agreed that both the Mastiff and the Bulldog probably had a common origin in the Alaunt. The Alaunt was defined in a dictionary published in 1632 as being like a Mastiff and serving butchers to bring in fierce oxen to keep them in their stalls.

An interesting note on Hounds, dated 1799, states that dogs in this classification may be described as follows: "first, the running Hounds which are used to chase hares etc., the Greyhounds, the Alaunts, or Bulldogs; these were chiefly used for hunting the boar. The Mastiff is also a good Hound for hunting the wild boar."

The word "Bulldog," with an approach to its modern spelling is not found in English literature until a relatively recent date. Ben Jonson, the playwright and poet, mentions both Bulldogs and Bear Dogs in his play *The Silent Woman* (1609). A second reference to Bulldogs, with a near-modern spelling, is found in a letter by Prestwich Eaton, dated 1631, which is now in the English Record Office. The letter requested several things, among them, "a good Mastive dogge, his case of bottles replenished with the best lickour, and two good Bulldoggs."

It is interesting to note that at this time Eaton makes a distinction between Bulldogs and Mastiffs. The French made a distinction between the two as early as 1537. We have reason to believe that the Bulldog was a very ancient and well-known breed in England long before Ben Jonson and Prestwich Eaton mentioned them by the name under which we know them today.

Down through the centuries, until a comparatively recent time, the name "Mastiff" has been applied indiscriminately to all large or massive dogs. This was especially true of the Mastiff proper and the Bulldog. To further demonstrate this point, Guy Miege in 1707 made the following statement: "Our Mastiffs, especially those we call Bulldogs, are of unmatchable courage. One of these dogs will fight anything alone, bear, tiger, or lion, and will not quit his hold till he gets the victory or loses his life."

The word Bandog also was used ambiguously and applied not to a distinct breed, but to all dogs that were usually kept chained up or in bonds.

Until comparatively recent times, there were few books published which were devoted to the subject of dogs, either in a generalized way or as pertained to specific breeds. The fact that there were no newspapers until the days of the Commonwealth is another factor to be considered in discussing the lack of early records regarding the Bulldog. Once newspapers were established, bull- and bear-baiting had become so commonplace that the subjects had very little news value, so it was seldom that they were ever mentioned in newspapers except in connection with some tragedy. We do find a number of references to the collapse of the old Bear Garden on the south bank of the Thames on a Sunday in January 1583. The amphitheatre was crowded with eager spectators—men, women, and children—many of whom lost their lives or were seriously injured.

In such records as do still exist today, early writers state that Bulldogs, like other races far removed from their primitive types, are difficult of reproduction; that the males are seldom amorous, and that the females frequently miscarry; that although their development is slow and they scarcely acquire maturity under eighteen months of age, their life span is short and at five or six years of age, Bulldogs exhibit signs of decay and decrepitude. The cerebral capacity of a Bulldog is smaller than that of many other breeds of dogs, and it was long the contention that for this reason the Bulldog was inferior in intelligence to other, larger, dogs.

The Bulldog took his name from his main function, which was to

15

attack the bull. Nothing exceeded the fury with which the Bulldog fell upon other animals, nor the tenacity with which he kept his hold. In attacking the bull, the dog always assailed his adversary in front and generally fastened his teeth on the bull's lip, tongue, or eye, where he held and hung on despite the most desperate efforts of the bull to free himself.

Whenever a Bulldog attacked any of the extremities, the action was invariably considered an indication of degeneracy from the original purity of the breed. Even puppies six months old would be encouraged to assail a bull, and thereby give decisive proof of the purity of their breeding. If permitted, they would suffer themselves to be destroyed rather than to relinquish the victory.

Such trials were sometimes made wth the whelps of a particular litter to show the purity of their descent, and to prove that there had been no improper cross by which the future fame of their posterity might be tarnished. However, they were seldom entered in a regular ring until they were from fifteen to eighteen months old. Their ligaments were not considered at full strength and hardness until they were two years old, and the most experienced breeders declared that the Bulldog did not reach his prime until he was five years of age.

The Bulldog seldom barked; some were known never to bark or scarcely even to growl or utter any kind of sound.

In the early part of the nineteenth century, Lord Orford decided that the Greyhound was deficient in courage and perseverance, and he set himself to rectify these faults. Selecting a Bulldog, one of the smooth, rat tail variety, Lord Orford used it as a cross with one of his Greyhound bitches. He kept the female whelps and crossed them with some of his fleetest Greyhounds. After the sixth or seventh generation, there was left not a vestige of the form of the Bulldog, but his courage and indomitable spirit remained. Having once started after game, these crossbred dogs would not abandon the chase until they fell or perhaps died.

The Roman Claudian (A. D. 395-404), describing "The British Hound that brings the bull's big forehead to the ground," said that the dog's courage and activity in attacking the bull were particularly commendable.

Symmachus, a contemporary of Claudian, mentioned seven Irish Bulldogs as the first produced in the Circus at Rome to the great

16

Bull-baiting probably got its start in England from the butchers' dogs' attempts at restraining livestock. Over the years and until it was abolished, bull-baiting became more formalized and a number of variations of the basic idea were developed.

Bull-Baiting
Reproduction of an oil painting probably by Charles Towne, circa 1800.

admiration of the people, who were so struck with the dogs' ferocity and boldness that it was universally imagined that the dogs were brought over in cages of iron.

England's James the First is known to have singled out one of his fiercest lions in the Tower and to have turned him loose upon a couple of Bulldogs. To the astonishment of the whole court, the dogs showed no signs of apprehension, did not decline the combat and even provoked it, sprang upon the lion, engaged him closely with an equal courage, and at last, in spite of all the lion's efforts, mastered him and threw him upon his back.

Thus we have a thumbnail sketch of the breed from its origin shrouded in antiquity to a point where we may with certainty say this is or that is a fact based upon recorded history.

Bull-Running

In order that we may better understand our Standard and the Bulldog as we find him today, it is probably well that we should dwell at some length on the uses to which the Bulldog has been put, as well as the history and origin of the breed. Let us consider first bull-running and later bull-baiting as they were practiced in England from the time of their introduction as sports until the time when they were outlawed.

Through many generations, the sport of bull-running was practiced with much spirit at Stamford, Lincolnshire, on St. Brice's Day, November 13th. It is quite possible that the custom was once an autumnal sacrifice connected with the appeasing of the spirits of the dead, or with some feast which was held after the harvest had been safely housed.

The first bull-running at Stamford is traditionally assigned to the year 1209, during the reign of King John, and is said to have had its origin in a very simple incident. Two bulls were found fighting in a field by some butchers who did their best to separate the animals, but in doing so, drove the infuriated animals onto the public highway. Pursued by the butchers' dogs, the bulls at once set off at a furious rate into the town, much to the alarm of the townspeople. The Earl of Warren, being on horseback and noticing the danger, rode in pursuit of the animals. After a most exciting chase, the Earl succeeded in bringing the bulls to bay and they were secured. The

18

Bull Broke Loose
From a colored engraving, artist unknown, circa 1820.

efforts to catch the bulls proved great sport to the noble huntsman, and so pleased was he, that he determined to perpetuate so prolific a source of amusement. He offered to the town, as a gift, the meadow in which the fight took place, on condition that a bull be provided each year for the purpose of being run to bay on St. Brice's Day.

An eyewitness described the scene on the occasion of a Stamford running as quite appalling to the sensitive mind. Persons of the baser sort flooded in from all the neighboring villages. Horse-jobbers, hostlers, cads, butchers, pig-jobbers, and men of such classes came together in large numbers and the town was delivered into their hands for the day. Then riot, yelling, and shouting of the worst sort held sway.

At the tolling of the bell, the bull was let loose from the dark shed in which he had been detained for the night. If his ferocity was not equal to the expectation of the mob, he was goaded to greater madness by all the arts which brutal natures could suggest or devise. Not infrequently the poor beast's flesh was lacerated and spirits poured into the wounds to further the bull's agonized efforts to gore the Bulldog, or at least to avoid his hold.

The objective of the bullards, after causing the bull to tear at a furious rate through the town, was to drive the frenzied animal onto the bridge where it was immediately surrounded and lifted bodily over the parapet, then plunged into the river below. If the bullards succeeded in accomplishing these things before twelve o'clock, they were entitled to another bull. Apparently it is from this custom of bull-running that the old saying arises: "Upon the turf, the bull was thrown over the bridge." (That is, a form of foul play was practiced.)

Bull-running at Tutbury in Staffordshire was a semi-religious custom carried out by the minstrels of Tutbury Castle. Here it was a church function whereby the church, through its Prior, annually gave the minstrels a bull to be run. This particular form of bull-running is supposed to have been instituted by John O'Gaunt (1340-1399), Duke of Lancaster, in imitation of the bull feast of Spain, the native country of the Queen, who resided for some time at the Castle of Tutbury. It appears to have formed, originally, the concluding scene of a festival held in the town and called "The Minstrels' Court." The more pleasing part of the festival had been long abandoned, although its cruel and revolting features survived for many years.

The Tutbury bull-running was carried out in the following manner: "After dinner all of the minstrels repaired to the Priory Gate in Tutbury, without any manner of weapons, attended the turning out of the bull, which the bailiff of the Manor was obliged to provide. The bull was to have the tips of his horns sawed off, his ears and tail cut off, his body smeared all over with soap, and his nose blown full of beaten pepper. Then the steward made a proclamation that all manner of persons except minstrels should give way to the bull, and not come within forty feet of him at their own peril, nor hinder the minstrels in their pursuit of him. After the proclamation, the Prior's bailiff turned the bull out among the minstrels, and if any of them could cut off a piece of the bull's skin before he ran into Derbyshire, the minstrel was known as the King of Music and the bull was his, but if the bull reached Derbyshire sound and uncut, he was the Lord Prior's again. If the bull was taken and a piece of him cut off, then he was brought to the bailiff's house and there collared and roped and so brought to the bull ring in the High Street at Tutbury. There he was baited with dogs, the first course in honor of the King of Music; the second, in honor of the Prior; the third, for the town; and if more, for the diversion of the spectators. After he was baited the King could dispose of him as he pleased."

This practice was altered in later years. The young men of Staffordshire, armed with sticks about a yard long, contended with the young men of Derbyshire, who were similarly armed; while one party tried to drive the bull into Derbyshire, the other attempted to keep him in Staffordshire. Many heads were broken in these contests.

Also in later years, the King of Music and the bailiff made a bargain—the bailiff gave the King five nobles (about $8.50) in lieu of his right to the bull and then sent the animal to the Duke of Devonshire's Manor of Hardwicke, to be fed and then given to the poor at Christmas.

Whereas one author states that the Stamford bull-running dates from time immemorial till 1839, bull-running was introduced at Tutbury about 1374 and was abolished in 1778. It is probable that bull-running was practiced only in three towns in England: Stamford in Lincolnshire, Tutbury in Staffordshire, and Tetbury in Gloucestershire. Bull-baiting, on the other hand, was common all over the country.

21

In formal baits, the bull wore a heavy collar and was tethered by a long, sturdy rope. The dogs were expected to attack from the front and attach themselves to the tender flesh of the bull's nose.

Bull-Baiting

During the Middle Ages, the sport of baiting was extremely popular in England and was patronized by all classes of people, from the highest to the lowest in the land. Almost every town and village in the country had its bull ring. The baiting of animals may be traced to an early period in English history. It was also a favorite form of amusement among the Egyptians, the Greeks, and the Romans, as well as the people of other ancient nations.

Bulls, bears, horses, and other animals were trained for baiting. This barbarous practice, the rise of which cannot be satisfactorily ascertained, had the sanction of high antiquity. Fitz-Stephen, who lived during the reign of Henry II and whose *Description of the City of London* was written in 1174, informs us that in the forenoon of every holiday during the winter season, the young Londoners were amused with boars opposed to each other in battle, or with bulls and full-grown bears baited by dogs. Asses, although they did not sufficiently answer the purpose of the sport, were occasionally treated with the same inhumanity, but the baiting of horses was never a general practice.

The original bull-baiting at Tutbury (probably at the Bankside Bear Garden) is thus described by John Houghton: "I'll say something of baiting the bull, which is by having a collar about his neck fastened to a thick rope about three, four, or five yards long, hung to a hook so fastened to a stake that it will turn around. With this the bull circulates to watch his enemy, which is a bull dog (commonly used for this sport), with a short nose, that his teeth may take the better hold. This dog if right, will creep upon his belly that he may, if possible get the bull by the nose, which the bull carefully tries to defend by laying it close to the ground, where his horns are also ready to do what in them lies to toss this dog; and this is true sport. But if more dogs than one come at once, or they come under his legs, he will, if he can, stamp their guts out.

"Dogs were sometimes tossed by bulls thirty if not fifty feet high, and when they were tossed either higher or lower the men about strived to catch them on their shoulders, lest the fall might mischief the dogs. They commonly laid sand about that if they fell it might be easier. Notwithstanding this great care, a great many dogs were killed, more had their limbs broken and some held so fast that by

23

the bull swinging them, their teeth were often broken out. Often the men were tossed as well as the dogs.

"One bull dog being tossed broke a leg in its fall. The leg was instantly spliced and the dog again, in that maimed condition, ran at the bull. Nothing but greater force than is in his power to exert could break the hold of the bull dog and he was endowed by nature. with the highest possible degree of courage.

"The custom was for owners of dogs who wished to bait the bull to each pay entrance fees and if their dog pinned the bull they received a prize. The reward might be five shillings, a gold laced hat, a silver watch, or an ornate dog collar.

"Many great wagers were laid on both sides and great journeys would men and dogs go on for such diversion."

As mentioned previously, the first bull-runnings in England were supposed to have been at Stamford in the year 1209, in the reign of King John, and at Tutbury in 1374. There are, however, grounds for the belief that bull-baiting began much earlier, and that it was probably first indulged in by butchers who employed their dogs to chase, catch, and throw the bulls, and to bait them so as to render the flesh tender. Moreover, Claudian's writings suggest that the practice of baiting bulls was a form of diversion in his time.

The incident which was mentioned in the previous chapter as involving the Earl of Warren in the supposed introduction of bull-running at Stamford, was described in a slightly different way in *Sporting Magazine* of March 1802 by an early writer who indicated that the episode resulted in the origin of the sport of bull-baiting rather than that of bull-running. His version of the incident is as follows: "William, Earl of Warren, Lord of this town, standing upon the walls of the castle saw two bulls fighting for a cow in the castle meadow, until all the butchers' dogs pursued one of the bulls (maddened with noise and multitude) clean through the town. This sight so pleased the Earl, that he gave the castle meadow where the bulls' duel began for a common to the butchers of the town after the first grass was mowed, on conditions that they should find a mad bull the day six weeks before Christmas Day, for the continuance of the sport forever."

This may or may not have been the origin of the old English sport of bull-baiting. At any rate, wherever it began, it became more

Bull-baiting had an avid following in England. All classes of society patronized the baits. Even though we tend to look upon bull-baiting as a repugnant practice today, it should be remembered that the demands of the bull ring infused into the Bulldog many of the breed's physical and temperamental qualities we admire today.

popular with the passing years. Its popularity created a demand for dogs qualified for the sport. These dogs were selected and bred for courage, power, and ferocity. From the thirteenth to the eighteenth centuries, bull-baiting was a national sport in England.

Among a number of informative stories about Bulldogs is one concerning a bait at Bristol in March 1822. An old and crippled bitch had been standing calmly at the side of a butcher watching the flight of the numerous dogs through the air as the bull cleverly and effectively disposed of his adversaries. At the command of the butcher, the bitch slowly hobbled into the ring. She was covered with scars, blind in one eye, and altogether deprived of the use of one of her hind legs. Unlike many good dogs, she did not run directly up to the bull's front, but sneaked cautiously around him, with her remaining eye vigilantly bent upon the bull's every motion, apparently watching for an opportunity to bolt in and grab the bull. This was rather un-Bulldog-like behavior, but considering the infirmity of the old bitch and the little chance of success she would have had if she had gone in like a strong, fleet, and unmaimed dog, it may have been in some measure excusable. She had pinned this same formidable bull about a dozen times, and she and the bull had slept many a night in the same stall. In the stable the two were as amicable as doves, but on the turf the situation was different. The bull's fiery and bloodshot eyes were fixed upon her the moment she made her appearance. He seemed to be perfectly aware of her capabilities and steadily kept his front toward her, turning as she turned and, disregarding all other objects, keeping his keen eyes fixed on her alone. Another dog unexpectedly burst into the ring while the two thus steadily eyed each other, but the bull sent him curvetting and gamboling over the heads of the spectators, without deigning to honor him with so much as a momentary glance.

It was some time before the bitch had an opportunity to get in close to the bull. At length she suddenly darted forward with a velocity of which she seemed incapable, and at one bound reached the bull's nose. Despite repeated attempts, she was unable to hold fast. Although her sturdy old friend tossed her off several times, disaster only tended to prove her invincible courage and she repeatedly went in to the old bull; at one time she managed to evade his horns so cleverly and grapple with him so stoutly, that it seemed she would eventually pin him. But he trod her off by main force, and running over her maimed body, left her to be picked up by her fond old master.

The following anecdote of a Bulldog bitch appeared in *Sporting Magazine*, January 1824: A butcher brought a bitch accompanied by her litter of puppies to a bull-bait. Upon letting the bitch loose, the butcher exclaimed, "Now gentlemen, I will say nothing of the goodness of this breed; you will see." Although she had scarcely a tooth in her head, the bitch immediately pinned the bull. The butcher then cut her to pieces with a hedge-bill, and she only quitted her hold with her last breath. There was instantly a great demand for her puppies which the butcher sold for five guineas apiece.

Another man, confident of the pure blood and intensive courage of his dog, proposed a trifling wager: that he would at four distinct intervals deprive the animal of one of his feet by amputation, and that after every individual deprivation, the dog, on his stumps, would continue to attack the bull. The dog attacked as his master had predicted. His master then called him off, and as soon as the dog had limped bleeding into his master's arms, cut off his head—certainly the more merciful action of the two.

One writer reports that he has seen a Bulldog pin an American bison and hold its nose down until the bison finally brought forward its hind feet and crushed the dog to death; the bison's muzzle, most dreadfully mangled, was torn out of the dog's fangs.

It was not uncommon to see the dogs at early English baits, with their entrails trailing on the ground, urged again and again to run at the bull they were baiting. In one case, a dog of great repute was gored by the bull so that his bowels were torn out. Securing them in their place with needle and thread, the spectators, in consequence of some wager depending upon the outcome of the baiting, then set the dog at the bull in this mangled and almost dying condition.

The following, a typical public notice, appeared in the *Weekly Journal*: "July 22, 1721, note: also a bear to be baited and a mad green bull to be turned loose in the Gaming-place; with fireworks all over him and a comet at his tail, and Bulldogs after him. A dog will be drawn up with fireworks after him in the middle of the yard; and an ass to be baited upon the same stage."

It was not unusual at a bull-bait to see a Bulldog, surrounded by fireworks, raised to a considerable height by a rope which was drawn up through a pulley arrangement. The dog maintained his position of safety above the flames by holding tight with his teeth to a piece of sponge attached to the end of the rope.

As an additional means of attracting spectators, boxing matches were sometimes held in conjunction with bull-baits. It is recorded that almost five thousand spectators witnessed an 1824 bull-bait which was followed by a boxing match.

In many towns the butchers were liable to a penalty if they sold the flesh of a bull in the market without having had the animal baited on the previous market day. The reason for this was that the flesh of a baited bull was universally considered more tender and nutritious than that of animals slaughtered without first being submitted to the process. The belief, while it does not excuse the brutality of the act, may have been founded on fact. The excited state of the animal just before death would have tended to hasten putrefaction, and the flesh would have had to be cooked sooner or it would have been unfit to eat. There can be little doubt that bull-baiting, as practiced by the early English, was not merely a cruel sport intended to gratify the lowest and basest passions, but also was intended as a means of rendering wholesome and nutritious a large quantity of flesh that otherwise would not have been utilized.

In the old Court Roll of the Manor at Barnard Castle, it is stated that "no butcher shall kill any bull two years old upwards, unless he first be brought to the ring and sufficiently baited." The ring in Barnard Castle (fixed in a large stone that was level with the pavement) was in the Market Place opposite the District Bank. Bulldogs of a strain known as "Lonsdales," named for Lonsdale, a butcher and publican who lived at Barnard Castle about 1780, were in demand for many years.

In 1802, after a very heated discussion, a bill to abolish bull-baiting was thrown out of the House of Commons. The practice continued until 1835 when it was made illegal by an Act of Parliament.

Bull-baiting continued to be practiced occasionally at the West Derby Wakes until about 1853, and baits were held at Wirksworth at late as 1838 or 1840. The last bull-bait in Aylesbury took place on September 26, 1821. At Ashborne the final bait was held in 1842, while at Lancashire the practice continued until about 1841 or 1842. It is interesting to note how many years passed after the Act of Parliament before the custom died out completely.

With the decline of bull-baiting, the number of purebred Bulldogs began to diminish rapidly. One early writer states that they were occasionally to be obtained in London and Birmingham and a few scattered places in the Black Country.

An engraving of Wasp, Child, and Billy, published May 15, 1809, bore the following account in the margin: "The above Bulldogs, the property of H. Boynton, Esq. originally of the late Duke of Hamilton's breed, and the only ones left of the blood, are in such high estimation that Mr. Boynton has received one hundred and twenty guineas for Billy, and twenty guineas for a whelp before taken from the bitch. It is asserted that they are the only real Bulldogs in existence, and upon their decease this species of dog may be considered as extinct."

The sport of dog-fighting, which succeeded bull-baiting in public fancy, was largely responsible for the diminishing number of purebred Bulldogs. Many breeders began crossing the Bulldog with the Terrier because they felt that such a cross produced a better fighter.

28

Bull-baiting portrays another chapter in the evolution of the breed as a sporting dog. And a survey of the facts surrounding the Bulldog's use for bull-baiting cannot but instill admiration for the courage and determination required of the breed in this old English sport.

Bear-Baiting

Few sports in England have been more popular than was bear-baiting during its heyday. The years from 1550 to about 1680 were the palmy period for bear-baiting, and during that time, the popularity of all other forms of amusement waned before its attractions. Because the baiting of bears was an expensive form of amusement, it was sponsored chiefly by the Courts. The responsibility for providing the bears for baiting was considered so important in those days of old that a "Bear Ward" was appointed for this purpose and was an official member of the Court staff.

Sir Walter Raleigh coupled the London Bear Garden, which was situated in Southwark, with Westminster Abbey as one of the nation's sights worthy to be shown to foreign visitors. The sport was much patronized in London but was by no means confined to the metropolis, for bear-baits were held in all parts of the country. From time to time during the sixteenth and seventeenth centuries, the royal bears were included in performances for the general public, affording an occasional view of the sport to the lower classes which could not themselves enter into the pastime as they did in some of the less expensive forms of baiting.

So far as recorded history permits us to form an opinion, we may assume that Edward III (Edward the Confessor), King of the Anglo-Saxons (1004-1006), was the first to introduce the Roman sport of bear-baiting into England. We must not lose sight of the possibility, however, that the Romans may have practiced bear-baiting during their occupation of England (55 B. C. to 350 A. D.).

During his visit to England in 1623, the Spanish Ambassador was much delighted with the bear-baiting at the Paris Garden "where they showed him all the pleasures they could both with bull, horse, and bear, besides jack asses and apes. They then turned a white bear into the Thames where the dogs baited him while swimming, which was the best sport of all." A later account of bear-baiting lists the

29

Bear-baiting is thought to have been introduced into England by the Romans. During its heyday bear-baiting was the most popular diversion in the country.

Ambassador from Morocco and the Duke of Albermarle as being among the many who witnessed the death of several dogs at the Bear Garden on March 3, 1682. One of the earliest accounts that mentions the Bear Garden at Paris Garden is by the poet Crowley, who wrote in 1550: "At Paris Garden each Sunday a man shall not fail to find two or three hundred for the Bear Ward's vale."

As bear-baiting came to be esteemed the highest form of sport in the country, some of the bears gained great personal notoriety as a result of their exhibitions of strength and individual prowess. One animal named "George Stone" flourished in the time of James I and was known from Hockley-in-the-Hole to Land's End for the "single combat" which ensured his fame.

In his *Merry Wives of Windsor*, Shakespeare mentions a bear which he called "Sackerson," and which no doubt enjoyed a reputation for proficiency and prowess in his time. During the days of James II, a third bear, known as "Young Blackface," belonging to an Irishman named O'Sullivan, fought the extraordinary number of twenty-two "single and double" contests in a single day against the best dogs in the country. This excellent champion was killed at last when he was matched against three dogs at once without his "protectors," as his iron collar was called, and which, as he always fought muzzled, formed a very efficient part of his defense.

Bear-baiting was suspened during the Plague. Then, deprived of Court patronage following the Revolution, the sport degenerated to the point where it was almost non-existent on a fashionable scale. It cannot be denied, however, that the public was loath to let it die out completely, and the Paris Garden was eclipsed in popularity from this point on by the new Bear Garden at Hockley-in-the-Hole, a part of Clerkenwell.

There are several references in old manuscripts and newspapers to a story of selling the Bible in order to purchase a bear for the annual bait. Presumably, this tale arose from an episode which occurred about 1612 at Congleton. There are several versions of the story, but one of the following seems the most probable: A new Bible was desired for the Chapel, and a sum of money was laid aside for the purchase. But the town bear had died just before the annual wakes, so the Bear Ward, being unable to purchase another, applied to the corporation for assistance. He was given the sum of money set aside for the purchase of the new Bible, leaving the minister to put up with the old one as well as he could.

Badger-baiting was still another of the blood sports that found acceptance in early English sporting circles. These contests were usually held in a *pit*, or similar enclosure. The string tied to the badger's tail allowed a handler to separate the contestants without injury to himself.

According to another version of the story, the Bear Ward was given the money realized from the sale of the old Bible. Still another story, but actually one that amounts to the same thing, was that the Bear Ward was given the old Bible to sell in order that he might have money with which to purchase a bear. Whatever the basis for the story, the scandalous tale was spread throughout the nation that at Congleton the word of God was sold for the purpose of obtaining money to buy a bear.

Congleton was not the only place reproached for selling the church Bible to enable the inhabitants to enjoy the pastime of bear-baiting. Two miles distant from Rugby is the village of Clifton where the church Bible was also said to have been sold for the same purpose.

Another story that has come down to us by popular tradition concerns the church wardens at Ecclesfield, where the bear stake was near the church yard. Supposedly, the church lacked the funds necessary to procure the bear for the annual bait which was a part of the feast, so these men pawned the Bible from the sacred desk in order to obtain the money to buy a bear. This story, too, is subject to question, for some accounts say that it occurred not at Ecclesfield but at Bradfield.

Until it was outlawed in 1835, bear-baiting remained a popular as well as a legal form of recreation. But by the end of the eighteenth century, this pastime—once the pleasure of kings and queens and the highest nobles in the land—was almost exclusively patronized by the working classes.

Badger-Baiting

Badger-baiting, too, was a good old English sport that was indulged in frequently and openly. The baits were attended numerously and supported with great earnestness by many who looked upon themselves (and were looked upon by others) as respectable men.

As late as the first quarter of the nineteenth century, the Axbridge Square was frequently the scene of cock-fights and badger-baits. In the latter, the badger was put into a box and the dogs were then expected to draw it, that is to drag it or worry it out of its shelter—no small feat when one considers that badger's formidable teeth and jaws.

The following is a first-hand description of how the badger was drawn: "You see, we put the badger into this long box with the door at one end. Then I stand by the box and open the door and he that backs the dog drops on one knee, holds him by the skin of the neck with his left hand and lets the dog in at the badger. The dog then catches hold if he is any good and the man pulls him out by the tail. The man puts the dog's tail in his mouth and gives it a grip, the dog lets go, the badger flys up as I pull him, and I give him a neat twist into the box again and slaps the door. That's what we call a draw."

A variation of badger-baiting was known as a "turn-loose." Here, the badger had a strong string tied to his tail and fastened to a ring in the floor. The badger had no protection (as he did in drawing) but with tooth and claw was forced to make the dog keep his guard.

Again we find the Bulldog-cross as well as the Bulldog used for a form of baiting, for it was customary about this time to cross the Terrier with the Bulldog, chiefly for the purpose of producing a dog better qualified for badger-baiting, but also for fighting.

Ratting

Ratting was another English sport popular during the early eighteen-hundreds. In this, the dog was expected to kill a given number of rats in a pit within a given length of time.

Probably the most celebrated of all rat killers was a Bulldog-Terrier cross named Billy, a dog that weighed twenty-seven pounds. He was bred and first owned by Charles Aistrop, but subsequently, Billy was sold to a man by the name of Charles Dew, who owned him during the greater part of his career. Billy's best record was attained when he killed one hundred rats in five and one-half minutes, and by the year 1825, he was reported to have killed nearly four thousand rats in about seventeen hours.

The first mention of Billy occurs in records made about 1819, when this hero of ratting history won a contest in which he was matched against a bitch, the property of a Quaker named Bowring. Then on May 13, 1821, the owner of a rat pit wagered a silver collar that Billy could not kill one hundred rats in twelve minutes. Unbelievable as it may sound, Billy not only accomplished this feat, but also managed to do it in less than the stipulated time, for he

Ratting, an essential activity several centuries ago, also found its way into English sporting establishments. Shown here is Billy, a celebrated rat-killing dog of the 19th century. He is depicted killing 100 rats in five and one-half minutes. The date was April 22, 1823.

A number of Bulldogs were matched against George Wombwell's lions in Warwickshire in 1825. Although several of the dogs were killed and most of the survivors were badly mauled, we must marvel at the courage of the dogs in facing such an obviously superior adversary.

required but eleven minutes to make an end to all the one hundred rats.

As late as December 12, 1824, Billy was still performing with his same incredible skill, consistently killing the one hundred rats without difficulty despite the fact that he had scarcely a tooth in his head and was blind in one eye. Probably to the joy of the rats, this celebrated canine hero died February 23, 1829, at the age of about thirteen years.

The sport of ratting actually was a service to society in that is disposed of a great number of rats, the carriers of many contagious and deadly diseases. And so again we find a sporting dog used for a sporting pastime that actually had some value beyond its recreational aspects.

Bulldogs and Lions

A contest between a lion and six Bulldogs was held in Warwick on July 26, 1825. In the account of the match, the den is described as being ten feet high and fifty-seven feet in circumference. The bars, of proportionate thickness, were spaced nine inches apart in order that the dogs might pass between them. The dogs, reported to be of the true Bulldog breed, were run at the lion three at a time.

Mr. George Wombwell, the lion's owner, was also its backer. Among the backers of the Bulldogs was Sam Wedgebury of Green Dragon Yard, Holborn, who was said to have had some of the finest Bulldogs in the kingdom. Four of Wedgebury's dogs, Turk, Captain, Billy, and Sweep, were used in the fight. Turk was killed in the contest and his skin was later stuffed. Captain, Billy, and Sweep all recovered from the conflict, although they required a great deal of nursing. Mr. Wombwell reported that his lion, Nero, showed no signs of punishment other than a few slight scratches on the lip.

Four days later, July 30, 1825, Mr. Wombwell's second lion, Wallace, was tried for courage. This contest also took place at Warwick, and the six dogs entered against Wallace were Tinker, Ball, Billy, Sweep, Turpin, and Tiger. In this encounter Tinker and Ball met the same fate as had Turk in the contest with Nero, while this second lion came through without a scratch.

37

Bulldogs and Monkeys

Between 1799 and 1822, Bulldogs were often matched against monkeys at the various pits in England. One of the earlier battles, between a Bulldog and a monkey named Jack, took place in Worcester in May of 1799. The wager was three guineas to one that the Bulldog would kill the monkey in five minutes. The owner of the dog agreed, however, to permit the monkey, which was reported to have been of medium size, to use a stick about a foot long as an added means of protection against the dog. Several hundred spectators assembled to witness the fight and the bets among them ran as high as ten to one in favor of the dog, which could hardly be held in. The owner of the monkey took from his pocket a thick round ruler about a foot long and threw it into the paw of the monkey. Then he said, "Now Jack, look sharp, mind the dog." "Here goes for your monkey," cried the owner, letting his dog loose. With the fierceness of a tiger the dog flew at the monkey. The monkey, with astonishing agility, sprang at least a yard high, and falling upon the dog, lay hold fast to the back of the neck with his teeth. He then seized one ear with his left paw to prevent the dog from turning to

Reproduction of the engraving *Tom and Jerry sporting their blunt on the phenomenon Monkey Jacco Macacco, at the Westminster Pit.*

38

bite. Taking advantage of this unexpected turn of events, Jack fell to beating the dog about the head with the ruler. So rapidly and so forcibly did the monkey beat, that the skull was soon fractured, and the dog, in a nearly lifeless state, had to be carried away.

What was probably the most famous and most widely advertised contest between a monkey and a dog occurred about 1822. In this contest, the white Bulldog-and-Terrier bitch Puss, owned by Tom Crib (the champion boxer), was matched against Jacco Macacco, a savage monkey that reputedly had the ability to kill any dog that was brought against him. By biting the jugular vein, the monkey had succeeded in killing his opponents in a good many of his previous encounters, which numbered fifteen in all. But Puss was not without reputation, also, for one author states that she had the courage to draw a badger from a blazing barrel of gun powder.

The contest held in Westminster Pit, a less reputable place than which could not have been selected. Nevertheless, it was here that some of the elite of society gathered to view the contest.

The wager was ten pounds to one that Puss, who weighed twenty pounds, would stay with Jacco for five minutes or kill him. This was a minute and a half longer than any dog had hitherto remained with the monkey, although some of the dogs previously matched had weighed as much as twenty-six pounds. After several minutes, a ring of blood began to form around the contestants. The crowd asked that the contest be called a draw, and this was done to the satisfaction of all.

Dog Fighting

By the latter part of the eighteenth century, dog fighting had become one of the principal forms of sport in England. Accounts of past fights and announcements of fights to come appeared in many of the newspapers. Usually the fights were held in pits surrounded by seats and boxes, but occasionally they took place in the open.

The general procedure for pit fighting was as follows: Each dog had a second who cared for him in the pit, and only the dogs and seconds were allowed to enter the pits. A line of string known as a "scratch" divided the pit through the center. The seconds would loose their dogs and let them fight until one turned away. The animals were then refreshed, and when "time" was called, the dog whose turn it was to go to "scratch" was sent across the line to engage his opponent. This procedure would be repeated again and again until the match was declared a draw or until one of the dogs refused to go to "scratch," was physically incapable of doing so, or was killed. Then his opponent would be declared the winner.

Most of the dogs used for fighting were Bulldogs or Bulldog-Terrier crosses. It was thought that a Terrier cross gave the dog more speed and agility, while the Bulldog element was believed to provide the necessary pluck, stamina, and endurance, for the matches sometimes lasted as long as two or three hours.

The following is a very interesting and instructive description of dog fighting at Copenhagen House in North London, following Mr. Orchard's tenancy in 1795. Copenhagen House was kept by a man called Tooth, who encouraged the brutal sport for the sake of the liquor he sold on such occasions. On a Sunday morning the courtyard was filled with Bulldogs and lounging ruffians who drank to intoxication. As many as fifty or sixty Bulldogs were to be seen tied to the benches at one time, while their masters drank and made match after match, at intervals going out to fight their dogs before the house amid the uproar of idlers attracted by the commotion. This continued throughout the afternoon, and then the mob dispersed. The residents of the vicinity were annoyed by the noise of the dogs and the yelling of their drunken masters returning home. To add to the commotion, bulls were baited in a common to the east of Copenhagen House.

In 1816, as a result of the repeated disturbances, Tooth was refused a license by the magistrates. Mr. Bath, who was granted the license, put an end to the nuisance by refusing to draw beer or offer refreshments to anyone who had a Bulldog at his heels. And a neighboring landholder took over the common and used it as a cow pasture.

A list of sporting houses where dog fighting took place included Tom Crib's establishment in Oxendon Street, Haymarket; one established in 1796 by Bill Ward—the oldest of the sporting houses; Tom Belcher's in Holborn; the Castle Tavern (also known as The Daffy), opened by Bob Grigson in 1809; The Hole-in-the-Wall; Long Acres; Horse and Trumpeter; Adam and Eve; The George; The Bear and Staff; the Plow; King's Head; The Sun; and The Brown Bear.

40

Dog Fighting
Reproduction of an 1811 colored etching, earliest known representation of the Westminster Pit.

Dog fighting became increasingly popular in the latter half of the eighteenth century. Because it was common practice to cross Bulldogs with terriers to produce pit dogs, the purebred Bulldog entered a serious decline and narrowly escaped total extinction.

Dog Fighting at the Westminster Pit
From a colored engraving, artist unknown, circa 1820

Of the notices which appeared in the newspapers of the time, the following one may be considered typical: "To the admirers of the old English sports, a great match will be fought at the Subscription Rat Pit, West Street, West Smithfield, on Thursday next, November 17, 1825, four sovereigns, between Rose and Boney, twenty-five pounds each, from the scratch, son to the old city Boney; to conclude with a match with two of the handsomest little Bull bitches in the fancy, of seventeen pounds each, from the scratch. Doors open at seven o'clock. The winner of the above will be open to fight any dog or bitch of its weight for fifty sovereigns at Mr. Reuche's Pit as above."

More than any other one thing, the sport of dog fighting was responsible for the fact that the purebred Bulldog was moving rapidly toward extinction. Although the Bulldog was highly prized as a cross with the Terrier, little if anything was done to preserve the breed in its purebred form. About this time, a number of laws were passed which placed restrictions and taxes on dogs; these, together with the fact that the Bulldog's chief uses were outlawed, all but completed his doom.

Fortunately, the Bulldog managed to survive, but rarely is he used for fighting today, although there are a few countries in which this sport is still practiced.

English and American Ch. Banshee of Beechlyn (Ch. Amrondine's Rockafella of Wiggin ex Strawbyn Silver Lining), owned by John O'Melveny and bred by Joseph Fox.

The Blueprint of the Bulldog

T HE first question that enters the mind of the owner of a Bull-dog, the prospective purchaser of a new dog, or the person contem-plating the merits of a puppy in a new litter, is: "How good is he?" This age-old question has been with us ever since Bulldogs first ran to bay the bulls in Lord Warren's castle meadows at Stamford, Eng-land, in 1209; probably it was with us a long time before that date, as well.

In view of the many varying opinions as to what constitutes a good dog, the question is not easily answered. However, it is not unanswerable. With the aid of this "Blueprint," a careful, intensive study of the official Bulldog Standard, and a point by point survey of the dog in question, the correct answer, unbiased and unprejud-iced, should be ascertainable.

First of all, we must rid ourselves of "kennel blindness." That is the ability to see each of our own dogs as champions, while the faults in dogs produced by other breeders are very obvious. After this first step has been accomplished, we must consider the Standard at some length. We must make a mental picture of the ideal dog described by the Standard, and then we must break him up and

45

Figure 1. Front View, Good

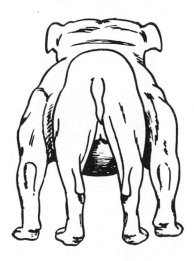

Figure 2. Rear View, Good

study him part by part, using both the official breed Standard and the drawings which illustrate this chapter to guide us in determining just what constitutes good conformation. For a clarification of the terms used for the various parts of the dog, see Figure 28.

In forming an opinion of any specimen of the breed, we must always remember that the general appearance (that is, the impression the dog as a whole makes on the judge) should be our first consideration. There should be no glaring faults. Nor should a dog be adjudged a good all-round specimen merely because he exhibits a single quality of super-excellence, yet is sorely lacking in many other respects. That is not meant to imply that we should not give just credit for a single superlative quality. But we must take care that we do not permit this one outstanding feature to blind us in our judgment of other parts of the dog which may be grossly lacking in merit.

The perfect Bulldog (and none has as yet existed) must be of medium size, about fifty pounds in weight, and have a smooth, glossy, healthy-looking coat. He must have a thickset, low-swung body; a massive, short-faced head; wide shoulders; and sturdy, heavy-bound limbs. The general appearance and attitude should suggest great stability, vigor, and strength. (See Figures 1, 2, 3, and 4). These attributes should be counterbalanced by the correct expression and behavior. The disposition should be tranquil and kind, resolute and courageous (never vicious or aggressive), and the demeanor should be pacific and dignified.

The dog's gait is of the greatest importance. The style and carriage of the Bulldog are peculiar. His gait is a loose-jointed, shuffling, sidewise motion, giving the "roll" characteristic of the breed. Few dogs today have this pronounced roll, but it is very much to be desired. The action should be unrestrained, free, and vigorous. Too many dogs hop along with a stilted gait on straight stifles (Figure 24), are cowhocked (Figure 27), or cross-paddle on weak pasterns (Figure 14).

One very capable judge told me not long ago that when he is judging a group of dogs in a show ring, he always gaits them first; any that are unable to move properly are excused, for he feels that correct gait is the first requisite of a really sound dog. I, too, feel that any dog with a very poor gait should be eliminated from competition.

Good conformation is of supreme importance (see Figures 1, 2, 3, and 4). The various parts of the dog which combine to constitute good conformation should bear a good relationship one to the other, no one feature being in such prominence, either from excess or lack of quality, that the dog appears deformed or poorly proportioned. For example, the head should be large, but not so large that the dog looks as if he will fall forward at any moment; neither should the head be so small that it appears to be stuck on shoulders that threaten to swallow it up at any moment.

In comparing specimens of different sex, due allowance should be made in favor of the bitches, for they do not manifest the characteristics of the breed to the same degree of intensity and grandeur as do the dogs. I find that most judges are reluctant to place a bitch over a dog, regardless of how good the bitch may be. In view of the definite statement in the Standard on this matter, I personally feel that a miscarriage of justice may result if the judge's final decision is swayed by the sex of the various exhibits. Most breeders who compete in shows try to secure for show specimens bitches that are doggy, with large heads, short deep bodies, and heavy bone. This type is difficult to find but is usually a sure winner. However, as a result of the way they are put together, they are not always good whelpers.

According to our Standard, the mature dog should weigh about fifty pounds and the mature bitch, about forty pounds. However, I would not penalize a dog or bitch for being ten pounds over these weights, as many of them are today. In England the weight stipulation has recently been revised upward, and is now sixty pounds for dogs and fifty-five pounds for bitches. Many judges, though, prefer medium-sized dogs and refuse to place among the winners either heavy-weight or light-weight specimens.

The coat should be straight, short, flat, close, fine of texture, smooth and glossy, and without curl, feather, or fringe. This description is easily understood, and one should have little trouble determining the excellence of the coat. Furthermore, most purebred Bulldogs will have the correct type of coat, provided they are properly groomed and well fed.

The color of the coat should be uniform, pure of its kind, and brilliant. The various colors found in the breed are to be given pref-

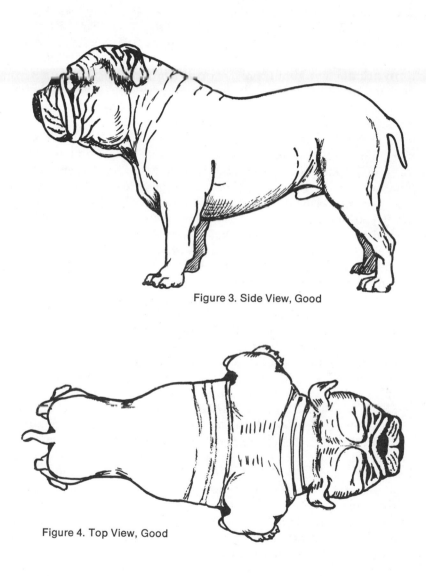

Figure 3. Side View, Good

Figure 4. Top View, Good

erence in the following order: (1) red brindle; (2) all other brindles; (3) solid white; (4) solid red, fawn, or fallow; (5) piebald; (6) inferior qualities of all of the foregoing. A perfect piebald is given preference over a muddy brindle or a defective solid color. All should have a black mask or muzzle.

Solid black is very undesirable, but not so objectionable if occurring to a moderate degree in piebald patches. It is very difficult to win in show competition with dogs that evidence any solid black.

In brindles and solid colors, a small white patch on the chest is not considered detrimental. In piebalds, the color patches should be well defined, of pure color, and symmetrically distributed. It is true that a few judges may have color preferences, but in the majority of cases, judges pay little attention to color, provided it is neither black nor blue. I feel that any advantage gained by color is due not to a conscious preference on the part of the judge, but rather, is the result of eye-appeal, quality of color, and perfection of markings. It has been my personal observation that rich red or fawn dogs with white markings are flashy and appealing to the eye, as are white and pied dogs, though to a somewhat lesser degree. This is especially true under poor lighting conditions. And in our section of the country, I have found there is a greater demand for fawn and white puppies than for any other color.

At this point, let us consider the drawings in Figures 1, 2, 3, and 4. Figure 1 shows a dog with a good front. The dog is wide, low, and heavy; his legs are straight; his shoulders are well placed; and the head is in proportion to the body, with a good under jaw, well-placed eyes, and the small rose ears which are so much to be desired.

In Figure 2 we have the same dog, but viewed from behind and showing a good stance, an overall well-put-together specimen.

Figure 3 is a side view of our ideal dog, showing conformation approaching the highest degree of perfection, and emphasizing the well-formed skull, the well-turned shoulders, roach, and brisket. The correct sourness of facial expression, proper stance, good bone, and correct tail placement are also in evidence, as are the good mush (or cushion), and rose ears, properly placed.

In Figure 4 we find the dog, as viewed from above, showing the typical and much-to-be-desired pear shape.

Now that we have a good, general, overall picture in mind, let us continue with the written Standard.

The skin should be soft and loose, especially at the head, neck, and shoulders. By taking the skin in the hand and pulling gently, one may test for the desired looseness and texture.

The head and face should be covered with heavy wrinkles and at the throat, from jaw to chest, there should be two loose, pendulous folds forming the dewlap. (See Figures 1, 3, 4, and 7.) "Heavy wrinkles" should not be interpreted to mean large, heavy, ropey wrinkles the size of a broom handle—the type to be seen now and then across the noses of Bulldogs of certain strains. This ropey wrinkling spoils the symmetry of the head and is a never-ending source of trouble; sores will form under this type of wrinkle because grime collects, stays moist, and has no way to dry out.

The skull should be very large, and in front of the ears the circumference of the head should at least equal the dog's height at the shoulders. Such a dimension must be considered as the absolute minimum. I personally prefer a skull at least a fourth larger in circumference than this minimum. (Figures 1, 2, 3, 4, and 7 illustrate correct skull proportion.) Viewed from the front, the head should appear very high from the corner of the lower jaw to the apex of the skull, and it should also be very square. The length from the apex of the skull to the lower jaw is very important, for this length gives reality to the square, brick shape that is demanded by the Standard. (See Figures 1 and 7.) Viewed from the side, the head should appear very high. It should be very short from the point of the nose to the occiput. (See Figures 3 and 13.)

The forehead should be flat, neither too prominent nor hanging over the face. Be very observant and make sure that the dog does not have a domed or a rounded skull (apple head), the type preferred in the Spaniel. The top line of the head between the ears should always be flat. (See Figures 1 and 7.)

The cheeks should be well rounded, protruding sideways and outward beyond the eyes, as pictured in Figures 1, 3, 4, and 7.

The temples, or frontal bones, should be very well defined, broad, square, and high, and causing a hollow or groove between the eyes. This indentation, or "stop," should be broad and deep, and extend up the middle of the forehead, dividing the head vertically, and being traceable to the top of the skull. Check the head studies in Figures 1 and 7. Note that the correctness of the stop is of major importance, particularly in relation to the other points of a really

51

good head. The old English custom of checking a dog's head is still a good means of determining its excellence. When a straightedge is so placed that one end touches the tip of the lower jaw (when the dog's mouth is closed) and the other end of the ruler extends to the top of the dog's head, the ruler should just barely rest on the tip of the nose, thus showing that all three parts are in a straight line.

The eyes, as seen from the front, should be situated low down in the skull, as far from the ears as possible, and their corners should be in a straight line at a right angle with the stop. The eyes should be quite in the front of the head and as wide apart as possible, provided their outer corners are within the outline of the cheeks when viewed from the front. (See Figures 1 and 7.)

The eyes should be quite round in form, of moderate size, neither sunken nor bulging, and in color they should be very dark. Avoid light eyes with a yellowish cast, as well as eyes that are very small or especially large. Eyes that are almost black are to be preferred, and when the dog is looking directly forward, the lids should show no haw and they should cover the white of the eyeballs.

The eyes are probably the most important single feature of the entire head assembly that makes for the good facial expression that is considered typical of the breed. The wide-set placement of the eyes gives to the dog his characteristic expression of honesty and sourness. Narrow eyes with any other placement destroy this desired expression, while large, goggle eyes with the whites showing are conducive to a "froggy" expression.

The ears should be set high in the head, with the front center edge of each ear joining the outline of the skull at the top back corner of the skull. Thus they are placed wide apart and as high and as far from the eyes as possible. (See Figures 1, 3, 4, and 7.) In size, the ears should be small and thin. The rose ear folds inward at its back lower edge and curves over, outward, and backward at the upper front edge, showing part of the inside of the burr.

A Bulldog's ears should never be carried erect, nor should they be buttoned or tulip. The ears should never be cropped or altered in any way. Occasionally we find ears that have been operated on in order to make them stand up. Usually this can be detected by close examination. It can also be detected by dropping something in front of the dog. If his ears have been operated upon, the dog will be unable to throw his ears when he is thus startled and the surgery

Figure 5. Erect Ears

Figure 6. Tulip Ears

Figure 7. Rose Ears, Good

Figure 8. Button Ears

Figure 9. Large Ears, Poor Carriage

will be readily detectable. Probably the most prevalent and objectionable type of faulty ear is the button ear, which completely destroys the dog's expression. (see Figure 8). Occasionally we find a dog with tulip ears (see Figure 6), but it is seldom that the bat ear or erect ear (see Figure 5) is encountered any more.

A common fault, and especially is this true of English Bulldogs, is the large thick ear (see Figure 9) which we see on a good many of the imported dogs. Many dogs with heavy ears are buttoned in some degree in one or both ears. With the possible exception of the eyes, the ears are the part of the head most important in creating the desired Bulldog expression. If a dog has bad ears he is seriously handicapped in competition, even though he may approach perfection in every other respect. For this reason, it is nearly impossible to win with any degree of consistency with a dog that lacks good ears.

Study Figure 5. Here we have a head study portraying the erect ears (pricked or bat) placed on a head that is outstanding in every other respect. Animals in their native state are always found with this type of ear. Because this type of ear carriage was common in the early Bulldogs (as evidenced by many early prints of the breed) the cropping of ears was a fairly common practice among breeders of fighting Bulldogs. While this type of ear is seldom seen anymore, I saw a Bulldog at a specialty show recently with ears as erect as those pictured here.

Figure 6 depicts the tulip ear, which represents the first step in the direction of the rose ear. This ear was also quite common among the early bull-baiting Bulldogs in England and represents not a malformation, but rather the evidence of an evolutionary movement toward our rose ear described in the Standard. At the same specialty show I mentioned, there was a perfect specimen of the tulip variety, and by coincidence, the dog with the tulip ears was in the same class with the Bulldog that had erect ears.

Figure 8 pictures the much-discussed button ear. This ear should not necessarily be considered malformed. Provided it is small and thin, it is merely an ear that is poorly carried. The button ear falls forward and down, destroying the dog's expression and giving the illusion that the skull is smaller than it actually is. However, it will be found in some instances that the button ear is malformed inasmuch as the ear is large and thick. This type of ear is not uncommon and is to be found on Bulldogs at almost any dog show of any size. In some dogs, only one ear is so affected, thus giving the dog a "goonish" expression.

Figure 9 illustrates (still on an otherwise good head) the large, thick ear placed high and carried poorly. This is not to be confused with the button ear. The forward carriage typical of the latter is not apparent, but the large thick ear is also one that spoils the neatness and expression of the head.

Figure 7, which for purposes of comparison is placed in the center of the drawing, is the highly prized, small, thin, rose ear that our Standard calls for. Note how in this illustration the ears are set on the head to good advantage. This correct placement tends to give the effect of increased size to the skull, and also gives the head expression and alertness. As I have stated before, nothing does so much for a Bulldog as good ears and good eyes, properly placed on the head. There is nothing plain or down faced in this specimen pictured in Figure 7. He has the expression we are searching for. The head is well proportioned, of proper size, and the under jaw is well formed with a good turn up. The dog's cushion is good and he is not snipey. The flews are well formed and cover the dog's tusks well. His wrinkles are his crowning feature, not overdone but well defined, completing a near perfect head.

The face (measured from the front of the cheekbone to the tip of the nose) should be very short, broad, turned upward, and deep from the corner of the eye to the corner of the mouth. The skin of the face should be well wrinkled, but, as I said before, the wrinkles across the nose should not be excessively large and ropey.

The nose should be large, broad, and black, and its tip should be set back deep between the eyes (see Figure 1, 3, 4, and 7). The nostrils should be wide, large, and black, with a well-defined line between them. Any nose other than black is considered objectionable, and Dudley (or flesh-colored) noses are absolutely disqualified from competition. The term "Dudley" dates back to 1877 to a magnificent, under fifty pounds specimen named Lord Dudley, who had this liver-colored pigmentation of the nose and lips. The fault was not outlawed at that time, and the dog was much used at stud, transmitting the fault to his progeny. Some strains show this faulty coloration of the nose and lips much more than do other strains, but "Dudleys" may result from any breeding. It should be stressed that "Dudleys" are disqualified from competition.

Many puppies are born with butterfly or parti-colored noses and some even with all flesh-colored noses, but usually after a few months such noses will turn black. The importance of large, black, deep-set noses with wide open nostrils cannot be overemphasized.

The chops, or "flews," should be thick, broad, pendant, and very deep, completely overhanging the lower jaw at each side. They should join the under lip in front and almost or quite cover the teeth, which should be scarcely noticeable when the mouth is closed. Well-formed flews help to give size to the head and accent its depth. (See Figures 1, 3, and 7.)

The jaws should be massive, very broad, square, and undershot—that is, with the lower jaw projecting considerably in front of the upper jaw and turning up. (See Figures 1, 3, 7, 12, and 13.) Today there are entirely too many dogs with malformed jaws. There are dogs with long narrow jaws and those with wry or twisted jaws; also, we are plagued with dogs that lack the outward curve and upward sweep of the lower jaw. (See Figures 10 and 11.)

The teeth should be large and strong, with the canine teeth or tusks wide apart, and the six small teeth in front, between the canines, in an even straight row. Many of our dogs today have these small teeth staggered in an uneven row; also, there are to be found too many dogs with the canine teeth placed too close together and the front teeth in an uneven row for lack of space to grow in properly. (See Figures 12 and 13.)

Let us study the jaws illustrated in Figure 10. This dog, while approaching perfection as to skull, and ear and eye placement, has an even bite. This is plainly shown by the fact that his teeth meet and are visible when the jaws are closed. This type of bite is to be avoided, for the Standard requires that the dog be undershot. While a perfectly even bite is seldom found, the almost-even bite is to be found occasionally. Either the perfectly even or almost-even bite detracts from the expression by producing a downfaced look and also destroys the upsweep of the lower jaw.

Figure 11 shows the wry jaw found cropping up from time to time in the breed. This fault is thought by many people to be inherent, while others feel it is a developed fault since few, if any, puppies are born with wry jaws. When a dog has a wry jaw, the under jaw is twisted to some varying degree, making it impossible for the dog to close the affected side of the jaw completely, and all or part of the

Figure 10. Even Bite,
No Turn-up

Figure 11. Wry Mouth or
Crooked Jaw

Figure 12. Correct Jaw,
Good Turn-up

Figure 13. Correct Jaw,
Good Turn-up

teeth will not meet. In many cases, the tusk on the lower side of the jaw will protrude beyond the lips when the mouth is closed. In many such cases the tongue falls out over the lower side of the jaw at the side of the mouth when the dog pants, rather than in front, which is the usual and normal way. This fault is considered very serious by some judges and may be penalized severely.

Figure 12 shows the correct jaw with a good upsweep, sound well-placed teeth and the undershot jaw which is necessary to produce a good upsweep and completely hide the small front teeth in the lower jaw when the dog (with the jaws closed) is viewed from the front. Note that the width between the tusks is filled in by the six front teeth which are in an even straight row.

Figure 13 is a side view of the dog in Figure 12, showing the continuous curvature of the under jawbone which completes the jaw placement and formation.

The neck should be short, very thick, deep and strong, and well arched at the back. A good neck goes a long way toward making a good dog. The neck must not be too short, as the dog's head will then appear to be between his shoulders; nor should the neck be too long, as this results in a "Setter look."

The neck should be covered with loose skin which should form a double dewlap from the lower jaw to the chest. It should be thick in proportion to its own length, and also in proportion to the size of the dog. The neck should have a pronounced arch from the withers to the back of the skull and should be very muscular (especially in males); in length the neck should be in a definite proportion to both the body and the head. (See Figures 3 and 4.) Too many long-necked, small-headed dogs are to be found. Avoid the dog that has either fault.

The shoulders should be muscular, very heavy, wide-spread, and standing outward, giving stability and great power. They should be broad, powerful, and sloping, with the appearance of being "tacked to each side of the body," to use the old English term for this correct type of structure. (See Figures 1, 3, and 17.)

The brisket and body should be very capacious, with full sides, well-rounded ribs, and should be very deep from the shoulders down to the lowest point, where the brisket joins the chest. The brisket should be well let down between the shoulders and forelegs, giving the dog a broad, low, short-legged appearance. The body should be

Figure 14.
Loose Shoulders
Weak Pasterns
Turned-out Feet
Fiddle or Chippendale Front
Light Bone

Figure 15.
Narrow Shoulders
Narrow Front
Light Bone
Hare Feet
High on Leg

Figure 16.
Narrow Shoulders
Light Shoulders
Crooked Legs
Splayed Feet

Figure 17.
Good Shoulders
Good Legs
Good Feet
Deep, Wide Front
Heavy Bone

well ribbed up behind, with the belly tucked up and not rotund. (See Figures 1, 3, 17, and 21.)

Figure 14 shows a faulty front with the loose shoulders that destroy the dog's gait, weak pasterns which let the feet turn out, together with crooked leg bones, creating a fiddle-fronted appearance on a dog that is also light in bone and hardly able to waddle along, much less have the ability to move with a decent Bulldog roll.

Figure 15, while seeming a bit unusual, constitutes a type encountered at many of our shows—with the possible exception of the hare feet, which are not as common as the other faults. This dog is narrow in the shoulders, a fault commonly coupled with light bone, poor feet, and a narrow, shallow front.

Figure 16 displays a set of narrow, light shoulders held up by crooked legs with splayed feet that have crooked nails. This dog has a very shallow brisket, giving the impression that the legs are long and the chest wide, an impression heightened by the crooked legs.

Figure 17 shows the good, well-turned shoulders, the straight legs with plenty of bone and good, sound, tight feet. This dog has a deep brisket and a wide deep chest to complete a very satisfying picture. This fellow couldn't cross-paddle if he wanted to.

The back should be short and strong, very broad at the shoulders, and comparatively narrow at the loins. There should be a slight fall in the back (close behind the shoulders) from which the spine should rise to the loin, then curve again more abruptly to the tail, forming an arch. This arch, which is termed roach-back or wheel back, is a very distinct feature of the breed. The back line, as viewed from the side, should give an impression of great strength, activity, and beauty, as illustrated in Figures 3 and 21.

Figure 18 illustrates the back, tail, and barrel of a dog with a fault that is called "camel back." This type may be seen from time to time in our show rings. The dog has the appearance of being humped up, with what should have been a roach thrown too far forward, and with too much slope down over the hindquarters. This dog has a passable rib spring, or barrel. The screw tail is not penalized, but neither is it preferred.

Figure 19 is the opposite of Figure 18, in that there is a decided dip in the back behind the shoulders, giving a kind of misplaced roach which is a complete departure from the true type. This dog is

60

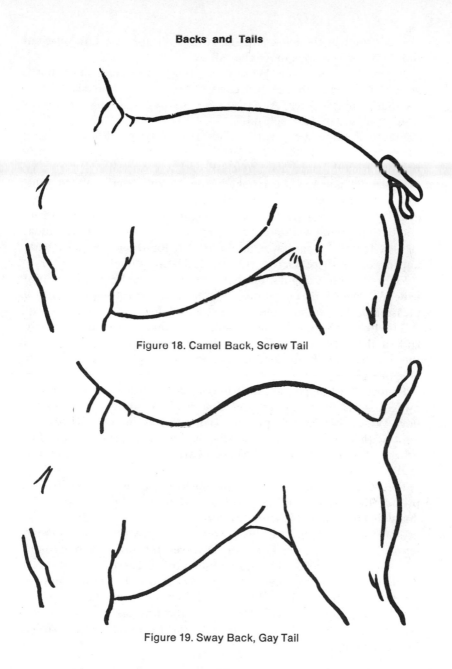

Figure 18. Camel Back, Screw Tail

Figure 19. Sway Back, Gay Tail

also cut high in the flank and has a high-set (or gay) tail. The tail should never be raised above the tail set.

Figure 20 pictures the dog with a straight back and a tail that is very high set, even though it is carried down. The impression is that the dog is long in back. Also, the stifle is straight, giving the dog an unnatural, square look behind.

Figure 21 shows a dog with a good rib spring; good hindquarters; correctly formed stifles; a low, well-set tail properly carried; a nice tuck-up at flank; and a good roach of back.

Figure 22 portrays the crooked stifle, found from time to time, which destroys the dog's gait and renders him a near-cripple. Dogs of this type are usually cowhocked. Figure 24 shows a stifle with no angulation, being without turn and very straight. This is not as great a fault as that shown in Figure 22, for the gait is somewhat improved, but there is a tendency toward being stilted.

Figure 23 shows angulation, balance, style, and the proper turn of stifle. All these things combined result in a good rolling gait with a pleasing profile and make for a good, sound dog.

The dog in Figure 25 has pigeon toes, that is, feet that turn in and spoil the leg line, making the legs appear bowed. As a result of the interference of the feet and the turn of the leg, this dog is incapable of a good gait.

Figure 27, while perhaps a little over done, illustrates cowhocks, a fault that is quite common and that tends to spoil the gait of the dog. When this fault is pronounced, there is interference of one hock with the other when the dog is moved at a brisk clip. The beauty of both gait and conformation are seriously impaired by this fault.

Figure 26 pictures a well put together hindquarter with the proper turn of stifle, and feet with a world of quality and style. This dog will gait well and is sound in every respect.

The forelegs should be short, very stout, straight and muscular, set wide apart with well-developed calves presenting a bowed-out line, but the bone of the legs should not be curved, nor the feet brought too close together. Always check a dog for straightness of the bones of the forelegs. The outward curve should be formed of muscles and not bone. If the bones of the forelegs are curved, the dog's action is seriously impaired. This fault is usually accompanied by crooked pasterns.

62

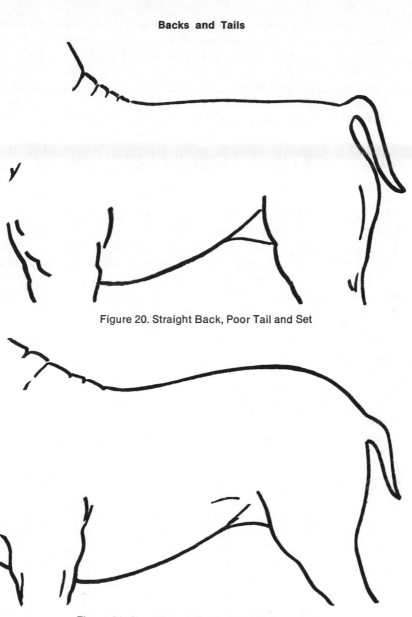

Figure 20. Straight Back, Poor Tail and Set

Figure 21. Good Roach Back, Good Tail and Set

63

The elbows should be low and should stand well out and loose from the body. To determine the comparative excellence of forelegs, and elbows, compare your dog with those illustrated in Figures 1, 2, 3, 4, and 17.

The hind legs should be strong and muscular, and longer than the forelegs, so as to elevate the loins above the shoulders. (See Figures 2, 3, 23, and 26.) The hocks should be slightly bent and well let down, so as to give length and strength from the loins to the hocks. The lower leg should be short, straight, and strong, with the stifles turned slightly outward and away from the body. The hocks are thereby made to approach each other, and the hind feet to turn outward. (See Figures 2, 3, 23, and 26.)

A very common defect found today is the straight stifle (as pictured in Figure 24). Also prevalent are cowhocks (as pictured in Figure 27). Either of these faults should be avoided as both tend to destroy the gait of the dog. He will have a stilted motion if the stifle is straight, or a weaving gait if he is cowhocked.

The feet should be moderate in size, compact, and firm set; the toes should be compact, well split up, with high knuckles and with short stubby nails. The front feet may be either straight or slightly out-turned, but the hind feet should be pointed outward. (See Figures 1, 2, 3, 17, 23, and 26.)

Regardless of the perfection of his other parts, the feet of any dog must be sound or he will be unable to cope with competition or even get around properly. Many times, bad feet are the result of neglect or lack of exercise. However, a malformed foot cannot be made perfect with any amount of care and exercise. But coupled with plenty of exercise, proper care of the nails (keeping the nails as short as possible at all times) is probably the greatest aid the dog owner can render to the development of good sound feet. The average dog's nails require periodic trimming and filing. Splayed feet, as pictured in Figure 16, are many times due to neglected, long nails.

The hare foot, or long narrow foot pictured in Figure 15, should never be tolerated in breeding animals. This fault is usually found in conjunction with narrow shoulders on the Terrier-type specimen.

The tail may be either straight or "screw" (but never curved or curled), and in any case must be short, hung low, with decided downward carriage, thick root, and fine tip. If straight, the tail should be cylindrical and of uniform taper. (See Figures 2, 4, 18, 21,

Side Rears

Figure 22. Crooked Stifle   Figure 23. Good Stifle   Figure 24. Straight Stifle

Rears

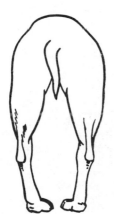 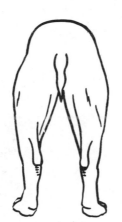 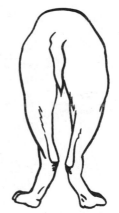

Figure 25. Pigeon Toed   Figure 26. Good Rear   Figure 27. Cowhocked

Figure 28. Parts of the Bulldog Labelled

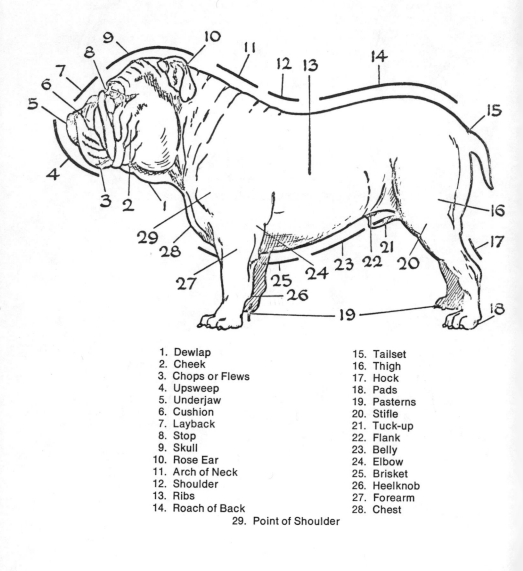

1. Dewlap
2. Cheek
3. Chops or Flews
4. Upsweep
5. Underjaw
6. Cushion
7. Layback
8. Stop
9. Skull
10. Rose Ear
11. Arch of Neck
12. Shoulder
13. Ribs
14. Roach of Back

15. Tailset
16. Thigh
17. Hock
18. Pads
19. Pasterns
20. Stifle
21. Tuck-up
22. Flank
23. Belly
24. Elbow
25. Brisket
26. Heelknob
27. Forearm
28. Chest

29. Point of Shoulder

23, and 26.) If "screw," the bend or kinks should be well defined; they may be abrupt or even knotty, but no portion of the member should be elevated above the base or root. A tail so elevated, known as a "gay tail," is pictured in Figure 19. A Bulldog's tail must never be docked. While the Standard does not indicate exactly how long a short tail may be, it is agreed by many judges and breeders that, at most, it should never be longer than the hock joint.

If you have followed the preceding steps carefully, one by one, and will from time to time review the procedure used in determining correctness of conformation, you will be able readily to distinguish between good dogs and poor ones. And you will be capable of spotting at once any superlative features as well as the more obvious faults.

And now you should be able to answer the question: "How good is he?"

Official Standard of the Bulldog

(Standard for excellence of type in the Bulldog, as adopted by The Bulldog Club of America, 1896, and approved by The American Kennel Club. Revised July 20, 1976.)

General Appearance, Attitude, Expression, etc.—The perfect Bulldog must be of medium size and smooth coat; with heavy, thick-set, low-swung body, massive short-faced head, wide shoulders and sturdy limbs. The general appearance and attitude should suggest great stability, vigor and strength. The disposition should be equable and kind, resolute and courageous (not vicious or aggressive), and demeanor should be pacific and dignified.

These attributes should be countenanced by the expression and behavior.

Gait—The style and carriage are peculiar, his gait being a loose-jointed, shuffling, sidewise motion, giving the characteristic "roll." The action must, however, be unrestrained, free and vigorous.

Proportion and Symmetry—The "points" should be well distributed and bear good relation one to the other, no feature being in such prominence from either excess or lack of quality that the animal appears deformed or ill-proportioned.

Influence of Sex—In comparison of specimens of different sex, due allowance should be made in favor of the bitches, which do not bear the characteristics of the breed to the same degree of perfection and grandeur as do the dogs.

Size—The size for mature dogs is about 50 pounds; for mature bitches about 40 pounds.

Coat—The coat should be straight, short, flat, close, of fine texture, smooth and glossy. (No fringe, feather or curl.)

Color of Coat—The color of coat should be uniform, pure of its kind and brilliant. The various colors found in the breed are to be preferred in the following order:
(1) Red Brindle, (2) all other brindles, (3) solid white, (4) solid red, fawn or fallow, (5) piebald, (6) inferior qualities of all the foregoing.
Note: A perfect piebald is preferable to a muddy brindle or defective solid color.
Solid black is very undesirable, but not so objectionable if occurring to a moderate degree in piebald patches. The brindles to be perfect should have a fine, even and equal distribution of the composite colors.
In brindles and solid colors a small white patch on the chest is not considered detrimental. In piebalds the color patches should be well defined, of pure color and symmetrically distributed.

Skin—The skin should be soft and loose, especially at the head, neck and shoulders.

Wrinkles and Dewlap—The head and face should be covered with heavy wrinkles, and at the throat, from jaw to chest, there should be two loose pendulous folds, forming the dewlap.

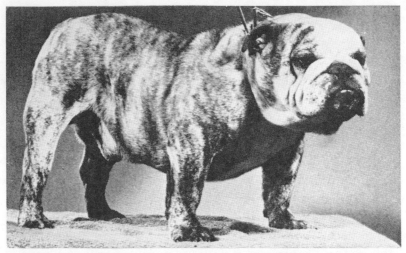

Ch. Ne Mac's Frankie O'Fearnought, owned by Ne Mac Kennels

Ch. Sir Reilly of Kilarney (Ch. Griff's Tardy Lad ex Zorro Torro Tamanita), owned by George E. Morris.

Skull—The skull should be very large, and in circumference, in front of the ears, should measure at least the height of the dog at the shoulders.

Viewed from the front, it should appear very high from the corner of the lower jaw to the apex of the skull, and also very broad and square. Viewed at the side, the head should appear very high, and very short from the point of the nose to occiput.

The forehead should be flat (not rounded or domed), neither too prominent nor overhanging the face.

Cheeks—The cheeks should be well rounded, protruding sideways and outward beyond the eyes.

Stop—The temples or frontal bones should be very well defined, broad, square and high, causing a hollow or groove between the eyes. This indentation, or stop, should be both broad and deep and extend up the middle of the forehead, dividing the head vertically, being traceable to the top of the skull.

Eyes and Eyelids—The eyes, seen from the front, should be situated low down in the skull, as far from the ears as possible, and their corners should be in a straight line at right angles with the stop. They should be quite in front of the head, as wide apart as possible, provided their outer corners are within the outline of the cheeks when viewed from the front.

They should be quite round in form, of moderate size, neither sunken nor bulging, and in color should be very dark.

The lids should cover the white of the eyeball, when the dog is looking directly forward, and the lid should show no "haw."

Ears—The ears should be set high in the head, the front inner edge of each ear joining the outline of the skull at the top back corner of skull, so as to place them as wide apart, and as high, and as far from the eyes as possible.

In size they should be small and thin. The shape termed "rose ear" is the most desirable. The rose ear folds inward at its back lower edge, the upper front edge curving over, outwards and backwards, showing part of the inside of the burr. (The ears should not

71

be carried erect or prick-eared or buttoned and should never be cropped.)

Face—The face, measured from the front of the cheekbone to the tip of the nose, should be extremely short, the muzzle being very short, broad, turned upwards and very deep from the corner of the eye to the corner of the mouth.

Nose—The nose should be large, broad and black, its tip being set back deeply between the eyes.

The distance from bottom of stop, between the eyes, to the tip of nose should be as short as possible and not exceed the length from the tip of nose to the edge of under lip.

The nostrils should be wide, large and black, with a well-defined line between them. Any nose other than black is objectionable and brown or liver colored nose shall disqualify.

Chops—The chops or "flews" should be thick, broad, pendant and very deep, completely overhanging the lower jaw at each side. They join the under lip in front and almost or quite cover the teeth, which should be scarcely noticeable when the mouth is closed.

Jaws—The jaws should be massive, very broad, square and "undershot," the lower jaw projecting considerably in front of the upper jaw and turning up.

Teeth—The teeth should be large and strong, with the canine teeth or tusks wide apart, and the six small teeth in front, between the canines, in an even, level row.

Neck—The neck should be short, very thick, deep and strong and well arched at the back.

Shoulders—The shoulders should be muscular, very heavy, widespread and slanting outward, giving stability and great power.

Chest—The chest should be very broad, deep and full.

Brisket and Body—The brisket and body should be very capacious, with full sides, well-rounded ribs and very deep from the shoulders down to its lowest part, where it joins the chest. It should be well let down between the shoulders and forelegs, giving the dog a broad, low, short-legged appearance.

The body should be well ribbed up behind with the belly tucked up and not rotund.

Back—The back should be short and strong, very broad at the shoulders and comparatively narrow at the loins. There should be a slight fall in the back, close behind the shoulders (its lowest part), whence the spine should rise to the loins (the top of which should be higher than the top of the shoulders), thence curving again more suddenly to the tail, forming an arch (a very distinctive feature of the breed), termed "roach back" or, more correctly, "wheel-back."

Forelegs—The forelegs should be short, very stout, straight and muscular, set wide apart, with well developed calves, presenting a bowed outline, but the bones of the legs should not be curved or bandy, nor the feet brought too close together.

Elbows—The elbows should be low and stand well out and loose from the body.

Hind Legs—The hind legs should be strong and muscular and longer than the forelegs, so as to elevate the loins above the shoulders.

Hocks should be slightly bent and well let down, so as to give length and strength from loins to hock.

The lower leg should be short, straight and strong, with the stifles turned slightly outward and away from the body. The hocks are thereby made to approach each other, and the hind feet to turn outward.

Feet—The feet should be moderate in size, compact and firmly set. Toes compact, well split up, with high knuckles and with short stubby nails.

The front feet may be straight or slightly out-turned, but the hind feet should be pointed well outward.

Tail—The tail may be either straight or "screwed" (but never

Morovian Newlo Bill.

English and American Ch. Marquis of the Hills.

curved or curly), and in any case must be short, hung low, with decided downward carriage, thick root and fine tip.

If straight, the tail should be cylindrical and of uniform taper.

If "screwed" the bends or kinks should be well defined, and they may be abrupt and even knotty, but no portion of the member should be elevated above the base or root.

	Points	
Proportion and Symmetry	5	
Attitude	3	
Expression	2	
Gait	3	
Size	3	
Coat	2	
Color of coat	4	
General properties	—	22
Skull	5	
Cheeks	2	
Stop	4	
Eyes and eyelids	3	
Ears	5	
Wrinkle	5	
Nose	6	
Chops	2	
Jaws	5	
Teeth	2	
Total, head	—	39
Neck	3	
Dewlap	2	
Shoulders	5	
Chest	3	
Ribs	3	
Brisket	2	
Belly	2	
Back	5	
Forelegs and elbows	4	
Hind legs	3	
Feet	3	
Tail	4	
Total, body, legs, etc.	—	39
Grand Total		100

DISQUALIFICATION

Brown or liver colored nose.

Ball, owned by Mr. Lovell and refered to in the Philo- Kuon Standard as having a tail approaching perfection.

The Philo-Kuon Standard of the British Bulldog (Canis Pugnax)

T HE British Bulldog is a majestic, ancient animal, very scarce, much maligned, and, as a rule, very little understood. If treated with kindness, often noticed, and frequently with his master, he is a quiet and tractable dog; but if kept chained up and little noticed, he becomes less sociable and docile and, if excited and made savage, he is a most dangerous animal.   He is generally an excellent guard, an extraordinary water dog, and very valuable to cross with Terriers, Pointers, Hounds, Greyhounds, etc., to give them courage and endurance. He is the boldest and most resolute of animals. The gamecock is a courageous bird, but he will only attack his own species; but there is nothing a good Bulldog will not attack, and ever brave and unappalled, with matchless courage, he will give up only with life itself. This noble dog becomes degenerate abroad—in truth he is a national animal and is perfectly identified with Old England —and he is a dog of which Englishmen may be proud.

PROPERTIES

No. 1   The HEAD should be large and high, that is, with elevation about the temples, and deeply sunken between the eyes, which indentation is termed "The Stop." This "Stop" should extend some distance up the head. The skin of the head should be wrinkled, and the cheeks should extend outwards well beyond the eyes. The forehead of the dog should not be prominent, as in the King Charles Spaniel, and not too round or it would be "Apple Headed." The head of a fine dog fifty pounds in weight, should measure round the thickest part about twenty inches.

No. 2   The EYES should be wide apart, almost black, of moderate size, rather full than otherwise, round, and not deeply set. The line of the eyes should be at right angles with the line of the face, and the eyes placed quite in front of the head, as far from the ear and as near the nose as possible.

No. 3   The EARS should be small, thin and wide apart. They should be either "Rose," "Button" or "Tulip." The Rose ear falls backwards, while the ends lap over outwards, exposing part of the inside. The Button ear differs from the Rose only in falling over forwards, which hides the interior. The Tulip ear is nearly erect. These are the only distinct sorts of ear, but there are various grades between them, and sometimes one almost merges into the other, for the dog does not always carry them in the same manner as, for instance, the ear which is naturally a Rose ear may become almost a Tulip ear when the animal is excited.

No. 4   The NOSTRILS should be wide and the nose large and almost between the eyes, and black, and deep—thus, taking the depth of the nose and the length from the eye to the end of the nose, the distance ought to be about the same. There should be a well defined line straight up between the nostrils. The best bred dogs will be liable to flesh or spotted noses; this is a blemish, but no sign of bad breeding; true bred Bulldogs will occasionally have flesh-coloured noses.

No. 5   The MUZZLE should be broad, deep, and short, with the skin deeply wrinkled and underhung, but not showing the

Ch. Sequel's Smasherjoe, owned by Mrs. A. R. Glass.

teeth; for if the mouth be even they are termed Shark-headed, which is considered a very bad point. The under jaw should be square and well upturned, with plenty of space in a nearly straight line for the six small front teeth in the lower jaw between the tusks. This is an important point, because it denotes width and squareness of under jaw.

No. 6 The NECK should be moderate in length, thick and arched at the back, with plenty of loose, wrinkled skin about the throat. The RIBS should be well rounded and the CHEST wide, deep and rounded. The TAIL should be inserted rather low down; thick where it joins the body, long and thin, and turned round at the end, in which case it is termed a "Ring" or "Tiger" tail, similar to that of the Greyhound but shorter. The perfect tail is shown in the print of Mr. Lovell's "Ball," and the tail nearest approaching that is the nearest to perfection. "The tail thin and taper, curling over the back or hanging down, termed 'Tiger'-tailed; rarely erected except when the passions of the animal are aroused."—*Vide Cynographia Brittannica*, A.D. 1800.

No. 7 The BACK should be short and arched in the loins, termed Roach-backed, wide across the shoulders and narrow across the loins. The Roach-back is shown in perfection in the print of "Crib and Rosa." Rosa's shape is perfect.

No. 8 The LEGS: The forelegs should be stout, with well marked calves, bowed outwards, short, and very wide apart. The hind legs should be slightly longer in proportion than the forelegs, so as to elevate the loins. The hocks should approach each other, which involves the stifles being turned outwards, and well rounded, which seems to obstruct the dog's speed in running, but is admirably adapted to progressive motion when combatting on his belly. The FEET should be moderately round; not so round as a Cat's nor so long as a Hare's feet, and should be well split up between the toes. The forefeet should be straight, and should show the knuckles well. The Pasterns should be strong, that the dog may walk well on his toes.

Ch. Westfield Flying Colors (Ch. Rawburn Avalanche ex Ch. Brookhollow
Gingerbush), owned by Charles A. and Virginia M. Westfield and bred by
Virginia M. Westfield and Brookhollow Kennels. This red and white male
has been the breed pacesetter for the past few years. Always owner-
handled he is a group and Best in Show winner as well as the holder of
numerous Specialty Bests of Breed including the parent event.

English and American Ch. Goulceby Craigatin Brave Boy, owned by Frank Haze Burch.

Ch. Lonarch Babbie. Photo courtesy of Mrs. A. R. Forbush.

No. 9 The COAT should be fine, short and close. The Bulldog has a very peculiar carriage, heavy and rather slow. He rolls very much in his gait, and generally runs rather sideways; his hind legs are seldom lifted very high, so that his hind feet (which, like the stifles, are turned outwards) appear to skim the ground.

No. 10 The COLOUR should be salmon, fallow, red, brindled, or white, with these colours variously pied. The salmon and fallow with black muzzles, called "Smuts," are choice colours. Some greatly admire the white, but a bright salmon with black muzzle would be the choicest of all colours. Black was formerly considered a good colour, but black and tan, and blue, are very bad colours. There is a strong resemblance between a brindled Bulldog and a striped Hyena.

No. 11 WEIGHT: A BULLDOG seldom weighs more than 60 lbs. If larger, he may be suspected of the Mastiff cross. On the other hand, he ought not to be less than 20 lbs. in weight, or he may be suspected of being crossed with the Terrier. The large Bulldogs are grander and more striking in their proportions than the small ones.

PHILO-KUON

LONDON
February 1865

Reproduction of a painting by J. C. Scanlan, circa 1836, depicting Ben White running his Bulldog "Tumbler" and Lady Sandwich's "Bess" at the head of Bill Gibbons' bull.

In bull-baiting if the dog was unlucky he could be, and often was, tossed high in the air after coming afoul of his opponent's horns.

The Standard and its Relation to Bull-Baiting

IN THIS era of dog shows, when Bulldog owners breed their dogs for exhibition instead of for combat as was formerly the case, there is a widespread belief that the Standard is designed merely as a guide for the judges and describes a purely artificial and modern concept of a show dog. While this may be true of the Standards of some of the modern breeds which from time to time become "fashionable" but which have never served any useful purpose in the past, it is emphatically not true of the Bulldog Standard.

With the advent of open dog shows in 1859, the need arose for some directive to give guidance both to exhibitors and judges, and something of the kind was attempted by the very astute Birmingham fancier, Jacob Lamphier, as early as 1864. But the first serious attempt to compile an authoritative description of the breed was initiated by the members of the original Bulldog Club (G.B.) in 1865 and known as the "Philo-Kuon Standard." It was intended to be an accurate—if somewhat idealized—description of a dog that, by reason of its peculiar bony and muscular structure, was perfectly

Ch. Taurus Trailblazer, (Ch. Steamboat of Kilarney ex Aries Annie Oakley), owned by Abe and Suzie Segal.

adapted for combat with the bull. The Bulldog Club members were eminently qualified for this task, for many of them had been born in an age when bull-baiting was a commonplace pastime, and some of them had even taken an active part in the diversion. Ten years later the present Bulldog Club (now incorporated) issued an improved Standard. This followed that of its predecessor rather closely, but aimed at tidying up the Bulldog, so to speak, so as to render him a more presentable animal for the show bench, *while at the same time carefully preserving all the really essential features of the old English Bulldog.* This is equally true of the Standard adopted by the Bulldog Club of America—in effect a paraphrase of the British version—as its title, "Standard for Excellence of Type in the Old English Bulldog, etc." bears witness. There have been minor revisions from time to time, which, apart from grammatical corrections, have resulted in only negligible departures from the original, with the sole exception that in Great Britain the permissible weight has recently been raised ten pounds. It is therefore true that, with very few reservations which amount to little more than dotting the i's and crossing the t's and which in no way affect the bony structure, our ruling Standards provide us with a fairly accurate word-picture of the old-time "business" Bulldog.

As an example of the reservations mentioned, take the case of ear formation and carriage. From the bull-baiting point of view this was quite unimportant. And since erect, or "tulip," ears and "button" ears were rightly deemed to detract from the animal's appearance, they have now been discarded in favor of "rose" ears. Both the former types were, however, permissible under the original Standard —and with good reason—since it was customary for those who "played" their dogs at a bull-bait to hold them by the ears while awaiting the signal to loose them for the attack. It would be no easy matter to hold a struggling, eager animal by the small rose ear that the Standard now requires! The rose ear is a comparatively recent introduction and consequently is not yet firmly fixed in the breed, which accounts for the occasional unwelcome appearance of button ears in our modern specimens. Moreover, the fact that puppies are usually born with button ears clearly shows that this formation is of very ancient origin.

Similarly, the tail served no useful purpose either in attack or defense against the bull, and those who revised the Standard were

Ch. Mapo's Patty, owned by Mapo Kennels.

Ch. Elvinar's Falstone Torpedo.

Ch. Souvenir, owned by Mrs. A. R. Glass.

88

fully justified in stipulating, *inter alia*, that it should be short and without any decided upward curve at the end. Look at the contemporary prints of old-time Bulldogs—notably that of Mr. Lovell's "Ball"—and it will be seen that the tails, although set on low, were almost invariably of the "pump-handle" type, that is, long and whippy, and turned up at the end. There was good reason for this feature, too, in the old days, since after many cumbersome and cruel expedients had been tried, it was found that the surest way to cause the dog to relax his vice-like grip on the bull, bear, or badger, was to bite sharply on his tail. This practice is often illustrated in prints depicting badger-baiting. Unpleasant though this must have been for both the parties concerned, it would have been infinitely more so in the case of the handler if it had been attempted on a short-tailed dog, or on one with a crank tail! In no sense, then, can either of these changes be said to have led to the creation of a dog that was not, in all its essentials, still a *Bulldog*.

It cannot be over-stressed that first and foremost in the minds of those who drafted the Standard was a determination to preserve those vital characteristics which, in the course of centuries, had been built up in the Bulldog, both by selection and by the inexorable operation of the law of the survival of the fittest. How well they succeeded we shall presently see, but it will be necessary first of all to have some understanding of the manner in which a bull-bait was conducted.

When a bull was to be baited, he was tethered by a strong rope, some fifteen or twenty feet in length, to a stake or ring firmly embedded in the ground. A swivel at the extremity of the rope allowed the animal to move freely in a circle. The tips of his horns were usually blunted, or padded in some manner, for it was not intended that he should gore his assailant, but merely toss him, so that the dog would suffer what an early commentator called "a damnable squelch" when he fell to the ground. As soon as he was securely staked a "game bull" (that is, one that had been carefully trained to the job, or who at least had some previous experience in baiting) would usually walk in a circle, pausing from time to time to scrape a shallow trench in the ground. This would afford some protection for his nose—the most tender part of his body and one that he knew only too well his enemy would endeavor to seize. Meanwhile, the "players" had taken up their positions at the perimeter of the ring where they held their dogs securely by the ears. At a given signal, one or more dogs were released, depending upon whether it was a "let-go" match or a "turn-loose" match. The bull, if he knew his business, having by now withdrawn to a point near the center of the ring where he had more freedom to maneuver, awaited the onslaught with watchful eye, his forelegs placed close together and his head lowered between them. A well-bred Bulldog invariably attacked the bull in front, and usually in perfect silence, as he made directly for the nose or lip. In making his run he endeavored to keep as close as possible to the ground (this was called "playing-low"), so as to get in under the bull's horns, the Bulldog's short forelegs and out-turned elbows facilitating this. If he failed in his objective, he ran great risk of being furiously trampled upon. On the other hand, the bull might succeed in slipping his horns under the dog's belly, and, with a seemingly effortless twist, send him soaring up into the air. The dog's owner or second now rushed in and attempted to break the animal's fall, either by receiving him on his shoulders or by allowing him to slide gently to the ground down long slanting poles. In some districts, too, the women would catch the descending animals in their aprons; it is said that at Totness in Devonshire, stout cloth was specially woven for that purpose. In the event, however, that all attempts at rescue failed, the poor animal might be killed outright from a broken neck or back. The "cloddy" specimens, short coupled, well ribbed up, with short thick necks and short backs, would stand the best chance of survival. More probably the dog would be only stunned, in which case he would lie "doggo" until he had recovered his wind, and then renew the assault with unabated fury. It is a curious fact, incidentally, that a bull will seldom attack dog or man when either is lying prone on the ground.

Supposing that the bull failed either to "lift" his opponent or to trample him underfoot, he instantly changed his tactics and assumed the defensive. Up went his head in a vain attempt to place it out of reach of his assailant, who simultaneously and with surprising agility sprang up to reach it. The dog was well served in this action by his muscular thighs and hind legs, which were long in proportion to the forelegs, as well as by the placement of his stifles, hocks, and pasterns, and by his arched loins. Moreover, the light hindquarters, small tucked-up belly, and shapely cut-up all played their part by relieving him of useless weight.

90

Sunday Evening with the Fancy.
probably 1840-1850

Lucy
From an engraving by Pyall, published 1834.

91

Ch. Welken's Pogo Morgare, owned by Virginia
McCreery. *Pogo*

Ch. Shauncy Duncan Dunce My
Mijo, owned by John and Sandy
Barrow. *Langdon*

Now, what if the Bulldog succeeded in pinning the bull? Seldom indeed, despite every strategem employed by the suffering animal—infuriated stampings and tramplings, violent tossings of the head, at one moment swinging his tormentor in the air and the next, beating his body against the ground—seldom did these frenzied efforts cause the dog to loosen his hold. The characteristic extension of the lower jaw beyond the upper allowed the dog, in running directly from the front (as all good Bulldogs do in making their attack) to grasp the muzzle with greater certainty than would be the case if the mouth were level, and gave a vise-like grip which was increased by the turn-up and the setting of the canine teeth in the wide and powerful jaws. A wry-jawed animal would have been shaken off in no time, and such a blemish is still rightly accounted a very serious fault.

The large head that the Standard requires, but which some believe to be the cause of so much trouble and mortality at parturition, has always been regarded as an essential Bulldog feature, though it may not be evident at first sight why this should be so. It can nevertheless be justified on two counts—namely, that the larger the head the greater the area for the attachment of those all important muscles that actuate the jaws; and further, who knows there

Ch. Dicken's Newlo's Golden Nymph, the first champion owned by Col. and Mrs. Bailey C. Hanes.

93

Ch. Royal Flasher, owned and bred by Mr. and Mrs. Herbert Grueber.

may not be some truth in the belief widely held by old-time fanciers, that "courageous animals all have the head behind and between the eyes, very large." After all, the one animal that can stand comparison with the Bulldog in point of courage—the gamecock—possesses this feature in a very marked degree. It is scarcely necessary to mention the well-known fact that the typical layback, with the consequent recession of the nose (furnished, as this should be, with large, open nostrils) allowed the dog to maintain his hold with such incredible persistence and without in the least impeding his breathing. If the jaws were level and the dog down faced, the rapidly swelling portion of the bull's flesh on which the Bulldog fastened, as well as his own upper lip, would be pressed against his nostrils; he would be unable to breathe freely and would soon be compelled to let go.

Blood now poured freely from the wound he had inflicted and the dog's face was bespattered with slimy froth. But he was not blinded, for the widely set eyes and the deep furrow between them served as a channel to draw the fluids away. The stop kept them from running over his nostrils; here they were diverted into the creases formed by the wrinkles of the foreface, and eventually they reached the dog's flews or chops, where they combined with his own sweat and saliva and dripped away from the extremities—just as the moisture drips from the hem of the linen hanging on the clothesline. This is the real purpose of the flews, and they are always more pronounced on animals that, like the Bulldog and the Bloodhound, were originally bred for battle.

At length the bull, overcome by pain and fatigue, though still resisting, sullenly lowered his great head to the ground. Until complete subjection was assured, the dog backed slowly, so as to avoid being trampled to death just as victory for him seemed certain. Here he relied on his powerful front and massive arched shoulders to keep his footing firm. And all the time he continued to shake and worry his wretched victim until, with a thunderous roar, the bull acknowledged his defeat, and unresisting, allowed the victor to drag him round the ring amid clamorous applause.

This ghastly recital gives only one side of the picture, for as often as not victory lay with Taurus, and a successful initial "pin," though half the battle, was not always the prelude to victory. It not infrequently happened that as the bull shook and tossed his head in frantic efforts to dislodge the aggressor, the piece of flesh that the

95

Ch. English Classic Barna-by Rudge and Ch. English Classic Julius Caesar.
Photo courtesy of Mr. and Mrs. Gilbert Peart.

Ch. McCreery's Tam O'Shaughnessy, owned by Richard and Virginia McCreery.

Ludwig.

dog had gripped was torn bodily out and the Bulldog fell with it to the ground, only to find retribution under his adversary's hoofs. This was more likely to happen in the case of very heavy dogs and particularly those which were "beefy" in their hindquarters, when they should have been "comparatively narrow at the loins," as the British Standard states.

In a very recent revision of the Bulldog Club (G.B.) Standard, the most desirable weight for a Bulldog has been raised from "about 50 lb.," as it used to be, to "55 lb." Surely this is a serious mistake and it is to be hoped that this is not merely the prelude to a further upgrading! Very heavy dogs are quite unsuitable for bull-baiting, as our ancestors were well aware. It is not only that they lack agility; excessive weight would almost certainly cause the flesh to which the dog fastened to be torn away, with the result we have just described —to say nothing of the almost certain destruction that would be the fate of a heavy animal when he came down "plomp" after having been tossed perhaps thirty or forty feet high.

There only remains the question of coat color. It is perhaps sufficient to say that the Standard has always condemned certain colors such as black, black and tan, and "blue." These were equally abhorred by the bull-baiters of old as being the outward and visible signs of impure blood. And no dog other than an out-and-out Bulldog can be relied upon to go straight for the bull's head.

In conclusion, if we have correctly interpreted the Standard in its relation to bull-baiting, what does it all really amount to? Surely just this: a judge will not go far wrong in placing the exhibits after he has examined them carefully in the light of these four vital questions: "Are the ears correct?" "Are the eyes dark?" "Is the tail according to Standard?" and, "Could this dog bait a bull?" It is no use retorting that he will never be called upon to do so. He *could* only do so if he conforms to the Standard and is, in fact, a *real old English Bulldog*.

Reproduction of the oil painting, *Portraits of Rosa and Crib, two celebrated Bull-Dogs, the property of a gentleman,* by Abraham Cooper, R. A.

Bulldog Bloodlines

I F YOU were to ask almost any Bulldog breeder which dogs he considers to be the Adam and Eve of the breed, you would undoubtedly be told, "Crib and Rosa." These two dogs, whose owner was H. Verelst, are the first, from point of whelping date (1817), mentioned in the English Kennel Club studbook. In evaluating their importance, one should also keep in mind the fact that Rosa was referred to in the original English Standard as being representative of all that a Bulldog should be.

Appropriately enough, Adam was the first Bulldog listed in the initial volume of the Kennel Club studbook. This dog, whelped in 1864, belonged to Mr. R. Heathfield, but was bred by Jacob Lamphier. While a number of others whelped in the fifties were also listed, the pedigrees of some of the early Bulldogs cannot be relied upon, for pedigree data was often recorded from memory long after the whelping date rather than being recorded immediately.

From a modern point of view, dogs whelped after 1850 are the ones that figure prominently in the pedigrees of our present-day Bulldogs. But in tracing pedigrees, a good deal of confusion is caused by the fact that so many dogs of the same breed bore similar names.

99

Crib, for instance, is a name which has been applied to nearly eighty known specimens. J. Hinck's Crib was also known as the "cropped" dog; Mr. G. Blewitt's Crib, as "Turk" and as Blackwall Crib; and Turton's Crib was also known as Sheffield Crib. Sometimes the name commonly applied to a dog constituted a description of the dog's outstanding feature (for example, the "cropped" dog), or the name might result from the locality in which his owner lived (for example, there were Bulldogs known as the Cremorne dog, the Kensington dog, and the Bristol Road dog). Often, the name of the owner, in the possessive case, was used as a prefix to the name of the dog itself. Thus, when a dog changed ownership, the name of the new owner was substituted for the name of the previous owner, compounding the original confusion caused by the similarity of the dogs' names.

In those early days there were all types of specimens, varying from very good to very poor. The small Bulldog was very popular in the 1850's and 1860's. In fact, at the earlier shows Bulldogs were divided by weight at twenty pounds and twenty-five pounds. In the Midlands, there were a number of black Bulldogs with pepper colored legs. While these were known as black-backed Bulldogs, the authenticity of their pedigrees has been questioned and it has been implied that they were not purebred specimens. The term "rough haired" was applied to some Bulldogs, but the term was not used as it is today, but rather was intended to describe a certain coarseness of coat on an animal that was still, technically speaking, a smooth haired dog.

Among the earlier Bulldogs, there are those that are known to posterity for other than show reasons. For instance, Mr. R. Lloyd Price's Michael the Archangel, after winning a prize at the Crystal Palace Show in 1870, was eaten during the siege of Paris the next year.

Ch. King Dick, owned by Jacob Lamphier, was the first great Bulldog on the show bench. This dog appeared at a time when the Bulldog, as a show dog, was just entering the sport. In addition to being the first great Bulldog on the show bench, Ch. King Dick was the first Bulldog to make a really great name in the stud annals and probably was the original pillar of the modern Bulldog world. Despite the fact that he was one of the earliest specimens of the breed exhibited, he was a first-class animal. As a stud dog he was

Old King Dick, the first Bulldog to complete his championship.

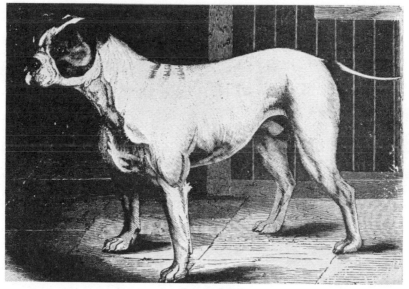

Jem Burns' Cribb.

Billy, Rose and Tumbler, owned by Frank Redmond, August 6, 1834.

Jem Burns' four pets, Jack Shepherd, Duchess, Cribb and Ball.

very successful and was responsible for the good points of many of the outstanding Bulldogs of later years, for he transmitted his sterling qualities to his progeny. His career may well be taken as a starting point from which has proceeded most of the successful strains of our latter-day Bulldogs. This dog was usually called "Old King Dick" to differentiate him from all the other "King Dicks" of later years.

Champion, or "Old," King Dick was whelped in 1858, the year prior to the first dog show, and he died in 1866. In addition to winning his title of champion, during his show career Ch. King Dick carried off a number of other prizes. Also, most of the successful prize strains of the present day trace back to him. He was the sire of Meg (the dam of Sir Anthony), and also King Dick II, who in his turn sired Michael the Archangel. The greatest of all his descendants, however, was the fabulous Ch. Crib, also known as Turton's or Sheffield Crib, who is regarded as the dog that, as a sire, has had the most profound influence on the breed.

That Ch. Crib was a direct descendant of Ch. King Dick on his dam's side there is no question, but the accuracy of his pedigree on his sire's side is a matter that never has been, and probably never will be, really cleared up. From the viewpoint of the history of the breed, this is to be regretted. Bred by Fred Lamphier (the son of Jacob Lamphier) of Sheffield, Ch. Crib was whelped in 1871. In the Kennel Club studbook it is stated that he was by Duke II ex Rush. His sire is also said to have been one of the various Tumblers, probably the dog of that name also known as Sheffield Tumbler, who was by King Dick II ex Slut II. Whatever may have been his parentage on his sire's side, Crib was certainly an outstanding specimen, and in the opinion of many good judges of the day, he was the best Bulldog that ever graced a show bench. Crib was a dog of over sixty pounds, a heavy-weight brindle, short in back and limbs without being in any way a cripple or monstrosity, but with an immense skull. This illustrious descendant of Ch. King Dick became one of the most celebrated show and stud dogs of all times, and died an unbeaten champion.

While there were many good dogs not bred from Ch. Crib, directly from Ch. Crib spring the four principal strains of present-day Bulldogs. The influence of Ch. Crib was enormous, and the dog's breeding became so fashionable that the four strains resulting

103

Wasp, Child and Billy.

The famous Bulldogs King Dick and Duchess. The dog peering through the gate is Venom (King Dick ex Duchess), August 29, 1863.

from Crib matings practically overran the show bench. And at the Bulldog Club Shows held at the Royal Aquarium in 1892 and 1893, every dog of known pedigree exhibited had Ch. Crib's blood in its veins.

It was in the late '70's that the influence of Ch. Crib began to show itself and the four great prize-winning strains were permanently established. The first strain is that which developed from the mating of Ch. Crib with Mr. Berrie's Rose; the second, from his mating with Mr. F. Lamphier's Meg ;the third, from his mating with Mr. P. Rust's Miss Smiff; and the fourth, from his union with Mr. W. Beckett's Kit.

The Crib-Rosa strain traces back to the mating which produced the outstanding litter containing Ch. Monarch, Ch. Gamester, Royal George, Britannia, and Blister. Ch. Monarch, a heavy-weight brindle with a white mark on his brisket, was the flyer of this litter which was whelped on September 17, 1878. Ch. Gamester, also a brindle, was not the equal of his famous brother, for he had a pair of bad ears. Despite this fault, Gamester was much used at stud and was able to acquire the title of champion. Royal George, a white and brindle Bulldog, was not a flyer, but he had the outstanding quality of a very fine under jaw, a point in which Monarch and Gamester were both deficient. Britannia, a bitch, was also an outstanding Bulldog.

The perpetuation of the Crib-Rosa strain in this litter was sustained by all three of the dogs. Monarch sired Ch. British Monarch, who was eventually purchased by Mr. Sam Woodiwiss. In order to secure Monarch, Mr. Woodiwiss paid the highest price given up to that time for any specimen of the breed. Monarch sired Ch. Britomartis and also Ch. Wheel of Fortune, both bitches that acquired enviable show records. He also sired Ch. Taurus, Monarch III, Young Monarch, and Nap. The latter was in turn the sire of Ch. Pathfinder.

Ch. British Monarch was the sire of Ch. Harper, Mr. S. J. Smith's Carrie, Sheffield Monarch, Queen Rose, German Monarch, and Little Bricks. Queen Rose was the best of the lot. German Monarch was a fair specimen only but was much used at stud, for his dam was the celebrated Ch. Dryad (originally known as Rosa Belle). Harper sired Heathen, sire of the great Ch. Monkey Brand.

Ch. Gamester perpetuated the strain by siring Ch. Diogenes, Ch.

105

Gladstonekoff, Bruce II (also known as Prince), the beautiful bitch Acme, Empress V, Bend'or, Blucher, Master Kildare, Dona Sol, and Maritana. The latter two were the foundation stock of the successful kennel of Mr. J. S. Pybus Sellon.

Ch. Bedgebury Lion (by The Alderman) was also a direct descendant of Ch. Gamester. Even as a puppy, Bedgebury Lion, a white and brindle marked dog, created a sensation. At nine months of age he was shown for the first time at the Bulldog Club Show at the Central Hall, Holborn, where his excellence of type set him decidedly apart from the other entries. After acquiring his championship in England, Bedgebury Lion was sent to America where he was owned by Mr. Trenor Park, then vice-president of the Bulldog Club of America.

Gamester's son Alaric performed a great service to the breed by siring Ashton Billy, Pagan, and Black Prince. The latter sired Kettering Jumbo, the sire of Mr. J. W. Ross' Salvo, a bitch of quality. Pagan sired King Orry, a dog noted for his marvelous head, who in turn sired Mr. Luke Crabtree's Ch. Boomerang (one of the best whelped to that date), Ch. Katerfelto, Ch. Facey Romford (sire of Forlorn '94), and President Carnot.

King Orry was owned by Mr. George R. Murrell, who kept a public house called "The Lion and the Lamb." Although unpretentious in appearance, this hostelry housed many famous Bulldogs, the most famous of which was King Orry. King Orry is often credited with having been the progenitor of a winning strain of Bulldogs, but from the foregoing it can be seen that his progeny actually constituted a continuation of the Crib-Rosa strain rather than a distinct strain apart from it.

Ch. Boomerang (King Orry's son) was the sire of Katapult, who in turn sired Ch. Prince Albert. From Ch. Prince Albert came a large number of winning dogs, and it has been declared that no other sire produced as many big winners. Prince Albert, a lightweight brindle with a good front, shoulders, and head, sired Ch. Kitty Royal, Ch. Broadlea Squire, Ch. Moston Roland, Mobberly Menestral, Moston Consort, Mersey King, Hazelmere Prince, Moston Duchess, Queen O'Scots, Lord Hesketh, and others. Among his progeny are many which have represented potent Bulldog breeding forces.

Mr. Murrell is credited as the breeder of Prince Albert, but actually, Mr. George Webber should be given credit. Mr. Webber owned Dame Fortune (a Dudley bitch) and mated her to Katapult. Through ill luck, Mr. Webber was forced to dispose of his dogs and sold Dame Fortune (then in whelp) to Mr. Murrell, who was subsequently credited as breeder of the resulting litter, although such was not actually the case. Just after Prince Albert came out, Mr. Luke Crabtree purchased him. Of all the good dogs Mr. Crabtree owned, none was the equal of Ch. Prince Albert, either as a winner or as a sire.

To return to the discussion of the Crib-Rosa mating, the third and last male, Royal George, sired Prince George, Adrastus, and Fisherman. This last-named dog, thought by many to be a monstrosity, was perhaps a little before his time and would have been a greater show winner and stud had he been whelped twenty years later. Adrastus, who had a good head but was said to have been deformed in front leg, sired Royal Rogue, the sire of Mr. C. F. W. Jackson's The Graven Image.

The Crib-Meg strain resulted from the mating of Ch. Crib with Fred Lamphier's Meg, a bitch of less than twenty pounds weight. This mating produced a strain of some of the best dogs to be seen on the show bench at that time. The litter resulting from the Crib-Meg mating contained the dog Tiger, a brindle, which was mated to Rush, a bitch owned by Fred Lamphier. The litter of four which resulted was made up of the dog Thunder, later renamed Ch. Richard Coeur de Lion; the dog Lightning, later renamed Duke; a third dog, Storm; and a bitch named Rain. Unfavorable publicity resulted when the litter was shown at the 1875 Nottingham Show where the judge, Mr. J. W. Berrie, charged that all four were faked —that they had been cut under the upper lip. Despite this charge (which apparently was never proved), Richard Coeur de Lion later became a champion and in addition, was the winner of many bench show honors. He was the sire of Beaconsfield, who in turned sired Ninepins and Thornfield. The latter was the sire of Mr. J. W. Baker's Aston Thornfield. Lightning became the property of Mr. Peace and under the name Duke won important prizes. Storm's career was cut short when he was poisoned. But we have no information as to Rain's fate.

Tiger also sired such outstanding dogs as Rosy Cross, Ch. Redowa, Ringleader, Mr. Clay's Duke, and Reeve's Crib. Reeve's Crib sired

Ch. British Monarch, an early English titleholder.

Don Leon (Don Carlos ex Lady Dudley), whelped in 1892.

108

Mr. J. S. P. Sellon's Ch. Queen Mab (who had a very outstanding show record), and Ch. Forceps. Ch. Forceps won a number of prizes and sired Ch. Blackberry, who was the dam of Mr. Woodiwiss' Ch. Baron Sedgemere, Ch. Boaz, and Ch. Battledora. Ch. Forceps also sired Mr. J. Davis' Lion Seeker, the sire of Mr. A. E. Baker's Aston Lion, who in turn sired Mr. J. W. Ross' Blackwall Beauty.

Another notable son of Ch. Crib ex Meg was Sir Anthony, a white dog, who sired such dogs as Ch. Rozelle, Slenderman, Doon Brae, and Ch. Billy (sire of Baby II).

The Crib-Miss Smiff strain resulted from a mating of Ch. Crib to P. Rust's Miss Smiff. The outstanding specimen from this breeding was Ch. Sancho Panza, a fawn dog, who in turn sired Ch. Lord Nelson. Lord Nelson sired Lady Nelson, a fallow-pied, and Empress II, a brindle and white, who became the dam of Ch. Diogenes. The latter's sire, it will be remembered, was Ch. Gamester, a son of the Crib-Rosa mating. Lord Nelson also sired Sir Garnet Wolsley, the sire of Cameron, who in his turn was the sire of Mr. C. G. Hopton's L'Ambassadeur, the first American-bred champion.

Julius Caesar (another son of Sancho Panza) was the sire of Lambkin. The fine qualities of the strain were passed on by Lambkin to his son Wadsley Jack, who continued the bloodline through his son John of the Funnels (owned by Mr. G. S. Mann), who was the sire of Walter Jefferies' great Ch. Rodney Stone.

Other outstanding progeny of Sancho Panza were Cervantes, Farewell, Don Quixote, and Captain Holdsworth's Faust. The latter sired Ch. Ida, owned by Mr. J. H. Ellis, who also owned Ch. Bellisima (a daughter of Ch. Sancho Panza).

The Crib-Kit strain was produced by the mating of Ch. Crib with W. Beckett's Kit and traced through their offspring Sepoy, owned by Vero Shaw. Sepoy sired Hudson's Dudley-nosed Sahib, who in turn sired Don Carlos and Don Pedro. Don Pedro sired such outstanding Bulldogs as Ch. Dryad, Ch. Don Salano (sire of Ch. Petramosse and Donna Venn), Ch. Kitty Cole, Ch. His Lordship, and Ch. Cigarette. Don Pedro also sired the great stud dog Stockwell, who sired Ch. Dimboola. In his turn Ch. Dimboola sired Walter Jefferies' Dick Swiveller, and the latter was the sire of True Type.

When Stockwell was mated with Blackberry (a daughter of Ch. Forceps), the resulting litter included Ch. Baron Sedgemere, Ch. Boaz, Ch. Battledora, and Barney Barnato.

The foregoing are the principal strains of Bulldogs which have produced our present specimens, for most of our dogs today can be traced back to Ch. Crib, or still further back to Ch. King Dick. However, there were a few outstanding specimens in the last part of the nineteenth century that probably did not belong to the King Dick or Crib strains. Of these, Sixpence (also known as Tramp), his son King Cole, and his grandson King Cole Junior (a dog sired by King Cole), represented three generations of outstanding Bulldogs and were used by a number of breeders as an outcross on the Crib strain. Both Ch. Alexander and Ch. Duke (the latter bred by the Duke of Hamilton) deserve mention as outstanding dogs not classified as members of the Crib strain.

Another cross-section strain known as Donaz was the result of combining the bloodlines of Don Pedro and Dandelion. Bulldogs of this strain possessed outstanding bodies. The Bapton Monarch strain was also a great favorite and left its mark on posterity. A Bapton Monarch son, Carthusian Cerberus, must be regarded as a particularly strong force among stud dogs. Carthusian Cerberus was a white dog bred by Mr. Cyril Jackson and later became the property of Mr. A. W. Vowles. This dog sired many hundreds of puppies in his day. A contemporary of Prince Albert (mentioned previously), Cerberus was equally successful in producing high-class stock. The combination of Cerberus and Prince Albert bitches, or Prince Albert and Cerberus bitches produced some of the outstanding Bulldogs of the time.

Ch. Kitty Royal, a thoroughly good all-round specimen, is an example of the result of breeding together a Carthusian Cerberus bitch and Prince Albert (the dam of Kitty Royal was Ch. Heywood Duchess, who was sired by Carthusian Cerberus). Jim Cerberus, another dog resulting from Prince Albert-Carthusian Cerberus bloodlines, was also an outstanding example of the great Bulldogs that resulted when these two famous bloodlines were intermingled.

Ch. Heywood Duchess and Ch. Muiravonside Lass have been cited in many instances as England's outstanding brood bitches of all time. Duchess, whelped in 1902, was bred by J. W. Kershaw. Her dam was Heywood Queen (a daughter of Ch. Katerfelto). Duchess was a heavy-weight fawn bitch with a very good head and extremely good spring of rib, and her influence was felt for many generations. In addition to Ch. Kitty Royal, among the famous get of Duchess

110

were Ch. Silent Duchess, Ch. Heywood Beauty, Mobberly Menestral, Bon Nefa, Heywood Marquis, and many other good Bulldogs.

Ch. Heywood Marquis, who was sired by Lord Roundcroft ex Ch. Heywood Duchess, has been cited as one of the most prolific sires of all time; 1,013 puppies are attributed to breedings wth this sire.

Another outstanding dog of the latter part of the nineteenth century was Ch. Bromley Crib, sired by Royal Duke ex Maid of Perth. Royal Duke, an Aston Lion son, sired a number of good Bulldogs before he was sent to America. Ch. Bromley Crib sired Swashbuckler, who in turn sired Moston Michael and Woodcote Sally Lunn. Swashbuckler, owned by Mr. A. Fergusson, had a great influence on the quality of the Bulldogs of his time, for he fortunately had the ability to pass on his good qualities and in addition was credited with correcting the tendency toward coarseness which had made its appearance among dogs of that period.

During the same period, the Stone strain was producing extraordinary Bulldogs. Stone-bred dogs, from the kennels of Walter Jefferies, were produced by inbreeding and were the descendants of Ch.

Ch. Basford British Mascot. Photo courtesy of Mrs. A. R. Forbush.

Ch. Rodney Stone.

Rodney Stone (the son of John of the Funnels, a dog rich in Sheffield blood). It will be readily seen that the new Stone strain was in reality a survival of the old Crib-King Dick bloodlines. Ch. Rodney Stone has been named as the most prepotent Bulldog that has ever existed, for his good qualities continued to appear in succeeding generations of his progeny. However, the forethought and care exercised by Walter Jefferies in planning the matings that produced the Stone-bred Bulldogs are factors that should not be overlooked.

Among the descendants of Ch. Rodney Stone that should be mentioned are Ch. Regal Stone, Buckstone, Lodestone, Ch. Rufus Stone, Lucy Stone, Buxom Stone, Ch. Lady Beowulf, British Stone, Royal Stone, Rex Stone, and John Campbell.

Another descendant of Ch. Rodney Stone was Parkholme Crib, who was sired by John Campbell. Parkholme Crib, bred by his owner, Mr. E. A. Vicary, was in his time acclaimed as the best living show and stud dog. As a sire, his fame was world-wide, his stock winning in Canada, the United States, South Africa, Austria, and Germany, and including such specimens as Parkhurst, Sunflower, Hever Vida, Tito Mattei (at one time considered the best headed dog in America), Luna de Gex, Scarlet Pimpernel, Sensation, Nuthurst Welcome, Nuthurst Surprise, Wroxham Nugget, Mcnella, Daisy Dumpling, Benfleet Crib, and many others.

Ch. Ivel Doctor, whelped November 23, 1895, was sired by General Roberts ex Ivel Nana. Ch. Ivel Doctor mated to Ch. Primula (who was also the dam of Parkholme Crib and many other winners of note) produced Ch. Nuthurst Doctor, who in his turn sired some exceptional stock. Ch. Nuthurst Doctor, the property of Mrs. Edgar Waterlow, was one of the best dogs of the period and won no less than twenty-five challenge certificates. Like his sire, Ch. Nuthurst Doctor was a good sound dog, and his son Ch. Nuthurst Lad was considered by some to have been an even better dog. In addition to the foregoing Bulldogs, Mrs. Waterlow had another very good specimen in Nuthurst Welcome.

Nuthurst Choice, a daughter of Nuthurst Doctor, became the dam of Nuthurst Ambition. These three Bulldogs, Nuthurst Doctor, Nuthurst Choice, and Nuthurst Ambition, represented three successive generations of Bulldogs having a distinct family resemblance in exceptional type, character, and physical form.

The Bulldogs discussed in this chapter constituted the basic breeding stock from which evolved the strains of the last decade of the nineteenth century and the many outstanding strains of the twentieth century.

During the latter years of the nineteenth century, the exportation of Bulldogs to America began to gain momentum, and the strains established to this point consequently followed two somewhat diverging paths, one representing the resultant strains in America, the other representing the more modern English strains. Therefore, the Bulldogs which subsequently became prominent pillars of the breed will be discussed in the two following chapters, "British Shows, Dogs and Fanciers," and "American Fanciers, Dogs and Shows."

English Ch. Roseville Blaze. She is considered by many to have probably been the greatest Bulldog bitch that ever lived.

British Shows, Dogs and Fanciers

THE first dog show ever to be held in England was at Newcastle in 1859, and had only four classes, which were for Pointers and Setters. Birmingham's first show, held in the same year, did not provide classes for Bulldogs either. In 1860, however, the Birmingham show allotted one class to Bulldogs, and the first prize (the only prize awarded) was won by a dog owned by Mr. J. Hincks.

At the North of England Exhibition held at Leeds in 1861 in conjunction with the meeting of the Royal Agricultural Society, a class with two prizes was provided for Bulldogs. At the Birmingham show held the same year, the entries in the Bulldog class were good enough to justify the awarding of extra first and second prizes.

Manchester held its first show in 1861, with one class provided for Bulldogs. In 1862 at the show held in the Agricultural Hall, London, two classes were provided: one for small-size specimens; the other for large-size dogs. The heavy-weight winner was Jacob Lamphier's King Dick. Bill George's Dan was awarded second place. H. Orme, with his Violet, was the winner of the small-size class.

The 1862 Birmigham show provided only one Bulldog class, which was won by King Dick. In 1863, the First Annual Grand

115

An oil painting by R. Marshall, 1855, of a dog show, at Jemmy Shaw's public house "The Queen's Head Tavern", London, 1855. This is probably the earliest known painting of a dog show, nearly 20 years before the Kennel Club was founded. History records that Jemmy Shaw, the proprietor in shirt-sleeves by the fireplace, was one of the originators of dog shows after the 1835 Act of Parliament prohibited "blood sports" in Great Britain. In 1852 he took over the "Queen's Head Tavern" on the death of the previous landlord, Jem Burns, a famous Bulldog breeder, who, like Shaw, had been a prize-fighter in his younger days. Previously Shaw had managed the "Blue Anchor", where he ran the "Toy Dog Club" and advertised his rat-killing terriers, where, in 1848, customers could see his "Tiny—the Wonder", a 5½ lb. English Toy Terrier, matched to kill 200 rats in three hours—winning the wager in 54 minutes. Unfortunately, the majority of the contemporary lettering on the back of the canvas of the painting is undecipherable and the names of the other fanciers are unknown, as are the dogs. Of the latter, at least eight different breeds are represented, one being the now extinct English White Terrier. The pictures on the walls including the famous engraving "Jem Burn's Four Pets" 1843, are more easily recognized than are the committee, or exhibitors, seated around the tables in harmony with their prize dogs of over 100 years ago.

from an article by Gerald Massey, Esq.

National Show was held in Cremorne, Chelsea. Two classes were provided for Bulldogs with the weight being divided at eighteen pounds. The class for heavy weights (over eighteen pounds) was won by King Dick, and the light-weight winner was Floss, owned by W. Tupper. In the same year, the first International Dog Show was held in Agricultural Hall. King Dick won the heavy-weight class and Violet won the light-weight class. (Classes at this were divided at twenty pounds).

Birmingham introduced a new classification in this year (1863) and provided separate classes for dogs and bitches. King Dick was again the winner in the dog class, and a bitch named Venom, also owned by Mr. Lamphier, was the winner in the bitch class. The following year at the second Cremorne show, two classes were opened to Bulldogs—Mr. Tupper's Brandy winning in the light-weight class and King Dick again being the heavy-weight winner.

The second International Dog Show, held at Agricultural Hall in 1864, provided two Bulldog classes, divided at twenty pounds, with Violet acquiring the honors in the light-weight class, and the undefeated King Dick taking the heavy-weight class. The Birmingham show in the same year divided its classes, providing one for dogs and another for bitches. King Dick again won in the dog class, and Mr. Lamphier's Madge won in the bitch class.

The Manchester show of this same year provided only one class for Bulldogs. It was won by Gambler, a dog owned by a Mr. Thomas.

By the year 1864, it had become evident to a large number of breeders and fanciers that a Bulldog club should be formed, and a Standard of Perfection should be drawn up as a guide for judge and breeder alike. The first Bulldog club was launched November 3, 1864, by Mr. R. S. Rockstro. Named The Bulldog Club, its stated objective was "the perpetuation and the improvement of the old English Bulldog." and the motto adopted was "Hold Fast." The only real contribution to the breed from this Club was the drafting of the Bulldog's description, which was known as the "Philo-Kuon Standard." Published in 1865, this Standard was by Samuel Wickens, who was then the treasurer of the Club. This first Bulldog Club was in existence only three years and never sponsored a show.

The third great International Dog Show was held at Agricultural Hall, Islington, in 1865 and provided for two Bulldog classes, dividing the weight at over and under twenty pounds. King Dick was awarded first prize in the heavyweight class, but no prizes were awarded in the light-weight division. At about this time, classes for Bulldogs began to increase, and the Birmingham Show in December 1865 provided a champion class (limited to dogs only) as well as classes for both dogs and bitches. King Dick won the champion class at this show. The Manchester show this same year provided two classes for Bulldogs, which were divided by weight at twelve pounds, and the same classifications were provided at this show in 1866. In 1867 the Birmingham show offered only two classes (one for dogs and one for bitches) as did Manchester in 1867, and both shows provided the same classes again in 1868.

In 1869, the National Dog Club held its first show at Islington and provided classes for dogs and bitches and also a mixed class for Bulldogs under twenty-four pounds. Birmingham and Manchester held to their old classifications, consisting of two groups of dogs.

The first Crystal Palace Show was held in 1870 with only two classes for Bulldogs, and Birmingham and Manchester also provided only two classes at their 1870 and 1871 shows. But in 1871, more classes were provided at the Crystal Palace show. It was in this year that Glasgow and Edinburgh held their first dog shows, each of which provided only one class for Bulldogs.

In 1872, the Dublin show had two classes for Bulldogs, and the second Glasgow and Edinburgh shows each had one class. The Crystal Palace Show in 1872 provided additional classes, and the Grand National Dog Show raised the divided weights class from twelve pounds to twenty-five pounds and provided two classes. Manchester had one class and the Birmingham show, two classes.

The Manchester show, and those held at Glasgow, Edinburgh, and Dublin in 1873, had only one class for Bulldogs. The Crystal Palace Show held that year provided the same classes as in the previous year, with the exception that the weight division was raised to thirty pounds. The Nottingham show held the same year had two classes for Bulldogs with the weight division at twenty-five pounds.

The Birmingham show in 1873 went all out and provided four classes for Bulldogs, one each for dogs over and under twenty-four pounds and for bitches over and under twenty pounds.

By 1874, the importation of Spanish Bulldogs, which weighed about one hundred pounds, threatened the continued existence of

Ch. Strawbyn Sheila.

Ch. Ultima Cleopatra.

Ch. Dunvegan Beauty.

119

the purebred English specimen. At this point, English Bulldog fanciers decided it was high time something be done, and a second Bulldog Club was organized. This second Club, actually the reconstituted Bulldog Club of a few years previous, came into existence in March 1875 in a London public house called "The Blue Post." Soon after the formation of the Club, a Standard of Perfection for the breed was written after a careful study of all available material pertaining to the breed. This Standard was published on May 27, 1875. The next task attempted by the Club was the devising of a table of points showing the relative values of the separate points mentioned in the Standard. This table was approved and adopted by the Club on August 5, 1875, and was published on September 2 of the same year. The Club also proposed that a studbook be compiled, but this was never accomplished.

The Standard drawn up and adopted by the Bulldog Club, with but a very few minor changes, is the same as the one used in England today. The two main points included in the original Standard but omitted in the present Standard are: the statement that the outline of Rosa in the well-known picture of Crib and Rosa was considered nearly to approach perfection in the shape, make, and size of the ideal Bulldog; and that no living specimens are now referred to as fairly representing the true type described and sought to be preserved as perfected. (It is of interest to note that for twenty years Rosa was considered as the perfection of form and figure in Bulldogs.)

The Club decided to have an annual show, which it still holds to the present day. The Club's first show was held in 1875 at "The Blue Post." There were ten or fifteen dogs entered and there were two classes—one for dogs and one for bitches. The dog class in this first show was won by Mr. Rogers' Nettle. Both dog and bitch were fawn-pied in color.

The second show was held in June 1876. Over one hundred entries were tendered, but a number of them arrived late and were rejected. The total entry was seventy-five Bulldogs owned by fifty-one exhibitors. There were five classes divided as follows: dogs over forty pounds; dogs under forty pounds; bitches any size; puppies, either dogs or bitches, under twelve months of age; and a selling class. A large percentage of the Bulldogs shown were good specimens.

Nearly two and one-half years elapsed between the second and third shows. Except during World War II this was the only time in the Club's history that one or more shows were not held annually. Interest in the Club had sunk to a very low ebb, but it was rejuvenated again in 1878 and the third show was held on November 2nd at Joe Hadley's Public House in Cecil Court, St. Martins Lane. The entries numbered sixty, and four classes were provided for dogs and bitches over and under forty pounds. There was no distinction made between the weights of dogs and bitches as is now the case. The four first place winners were Mr. Verrinder's Slenderman; Captain Holdsworth's Doon Brea; Mr. Harry Layton's Venom; and Mr. W. Oliver's Rozelle. It is noteworthy that the entry in the bitch class under forty pounds included twenty-five Bulldogs.

In 1879 the Club adopted a policy, which has continued to the present time, of supporting the Bulldog classes at shows all over the country with a view to creating interest in Bulldogs and inducing other fanciers to take up the breed.

The Club's fourth show, the first to extend over a three-day period, was held on May 15, 16, and 17, 1879. The entries totaled seventy-five dogs. Dual judging was attempted at this show, but proved to be a failure. The Club held a second show, December 9, 10, and 11, the same year (this was the first time the Club attempted to stage more than one show in a single year). The entries numbered seventy-six, and the quality of the entries was considered to be very high. Ten classes were provided, and included in competition were such typical specimens of the day as Gamester, Royal George, and Britannia.

On May 17, 1894, the Club became incorporated and has been known from that day until the present time as The Bulldog Club, Incorporated. This Club has the distinction of being the oldest specialty breed club in the world, having been founded in 1875 and operated continuously ever since.

Of the old-time Bulldog, little can be said in the way of praise. He was a dog that for generation after generation was trained to be ferocious and savage; without this ferocity, he would have been incapable of performing the tasks for which he was bred—namely, bear-baiting, bull-baiting, and fighting other dogs. That the Bulldog was well suited and prepared for these sports can scarcely be denied.

As a natural sequence when the Bulldog was no longer in demand

121

for the purpose of sport, the breed began to show signs of decline with a very distinct possibility of becoming extinct. At that time there was little interest in the breed among the wealthy, and a great deal of credit is due the English working man for the part he played in the preservation of the Bulldog. Gradually, the Bulldog began to gain in popularity, not as a fighting dog, but as a show dog and a companion, and a number of men became interested in keeping alive the great breed of dogs which had played such an interesting role in the history of England. It was the desire of these men to develop a Bulldog that was docile, obedient, and trustworthy. And it was the beginning of the changes wrought by these early breeders that made it possible for us to have our modern Bulldog, now regarded by most authorities as among the best natured of the canine family.

Frank Redmond, a noted breeder in the first half of the nineteenth century, probably did more than any other man to raise the standard of the breed, which from 1800 to 1830 had fallen to a very low ebb. Dogs named Bowler, Romdry, and Old Crib were the property of Mr. Redmond. He was also the owner of Billy, Rose, and Tumbler.

Ben White was a typical dog breeder, dealer, and keeper of fighting Bulldogs. He was probably the last member of the old school of the fancy in London who made dealing in dogs his main business. His preference was the Bowler strain. Edward ("Teddy") Morgan was another fancier of the old school, as were Ned Probert and Joseph ("Fakey Joe") Taylor.

Bill George, "The Nobby West End Butcher," father of the well-known judge, Alfred George, succeeded Ben White in the dog-dealing business after the latter's death in 1838. This business he carried on in such a manner that he became noted as an honorable dealer. Although he also had dogs of other breeds, he was probably the most famous Bulldog breeder of his day; it was in the Bulldog breed that he specialized, and he bred and possessed many good specimens. When dog shows became the vogue, Mr. George's kennel included some of the finest dogs of the day. Among the well-known Bulldogs he owned were Viper, Wasp, Ringer, Ajax, Lola Montes, Young King Dick, and Dan. The latter, a dog that weighed sixty pounds, was sold for $500.00, a very large sum in those days. Young King Dick was bred by Jacob Lamphier, sold to Bill George, and later repurchased by Mr. Lamphier for $200.00, also a fancy price in those days.

Jacob Lamphier, father of the fancier and breeder Fred Lamphier, was the owner of King Dick, K.C.S.B. 2633, the first Bulldog to attain championship status in England. King Dick, who was whelped in 1858 and died in 1866, was a red smut dog sired by Tommy ex Slut, and, as mentioned previously, acquired his championship at the Birmingham National Dog Show in 1865.

One of the very first men to take up the showing of Bulldogs, Jacob Lamphier was also credited with writing the first Standard for judging Bulldogs. Mr. Lamphier bred King Dick, Venom, Meg, Madge, Romanie, and Adam. The latter was the first Bulldog registered in the English Kennel Club studbook. To avoid confusion it should be pointed out that the aforementioned Venom was not the celebrated champion by that name, nor was the King Dick bred by Lamphier the Ch. Old King Dick which Lamphier owned.

Although other towns did boast of Bulldog fanciers who bred successful show dogs, London, Birmingham, and Sheffield were the main centers of Bulldog breeding activities during the period when dog shows (as we know them now) were first in vogue. Of the London fanciers, two were outstandingly conspicuous—Mr. J. W. Berrie and Mr. Verrinder. One of the earliest prize-winners bred by Mr. Berrie was "Old" King Cole (not to be confused with the King Cole of later years also bred by Mr. Berrie). Mr. Berrie also bred Ch. Venom, Ch. Monarch, Ch. Gamester, Britannia, Berrie, Blackwall Crib (better known as Blewitt's Crib), Jess, Cervantes, Ch. Blackwall Beauty, and many others. Mr. Verrinder in the sixties bred such prize-winners as Poll and Nosegay, and in the seventies he bred a number of successful show Bulldogs, among them Bill Sykes and Fagin (a white and brindle dog), Slenderman, Young Sir Anthony, Mona, and Rose. Ned Clarke and Harry Layton also owned and bred a number of good specimens. Among the best bred by Mr. Layton was Ch. Smasher.

Mr. Jack Ashburne (also known as "City" Jack), another London fancier, prided himself in being one of the old school, and bred Gun, Clicquot, Warrior, Madame Lola, and Ada, all prize-winners. Other London breeders were Mr. Crafer, Frank Redmond, Mr. Stockdale, Billy Page, W. Newton (who bred Peerless, and in conjunction with Mr. P. Rust bred Adrastus), James Goode, Teddy Morgan, Robert Fulton, G. Sandle, E. Nichols, Rivers Wilson, Jim Ferriman, W. H. Tyzer, and Edwin Farquharson.

Tom Ball, then of Peckham, bred Lord Nelson, Othello, and

Bonnie Bessie. He was the breeder of Ch. His Lordship, and Ch. Cigarette, but parted with their dam before these two dogs were whelped.

In the sixties and seventies, the principal Birmingham breeders were J. Hincks, E. Booth, Jesse Oswell, G. A. Dawes, and Fred Reeves. Other Birmingham breeders were J. Guymer, G. Underhill, E. A. Wilkinson, and J. B. Wilkes, all of whom bred winners.

In Sheffield, the most outstanding of the many who cultivated the breed was Jacob Lamphier's son, Fred Lamphier. He bred numerous prize-winning dogs including Rush, Queen Bess, Minnie, Gipsy Queen, and Duchess. Other Sheffield breeders were Tommy Barber, George Mosley, Peter Wilson, Tom Spencer, T. Nuttall, and Thomas Turton (who became the owner of Ch. Crib). Among the very old Sheffield fanciers who bred Bulldogs before the dog-show days were Jim and Tom Gibbons. Later, Joseph Taylor (known to his friends as Fakey Joe) owned and bred a number of outstanding specimens of the breed.

At Manchester was Mr. Henshall, who bred Duke III, Peg, and Julius Caesar. At Ipswich, Mr. W. Webb bred Meagre's Bismarck, Faust, and Ch. Ida. Joseph Bowman was another well-known Ipswich breeder, as was Mr. P. Rust who bred such notable specimens of the day as Master Gully, Ch. Sancho Panza, Lulu, Guppy, Ch. Diogenes, and Draco.

Mr. J. C. Lyell of Dundee bred Leeb, and later Ch. Britomartis. And in 1867, the Duke of Hamilton bred Ch. Duke.

All these fanciers were enthusiastic supporters of the Bulldog during the early days of dog shows, and their main objective was to produce a Bulldog that was better from a show point of view than any previously bred. As time passed, the number of fanciers increased, but their primary purpose, improving the breed, remained the same.

Mr. Robert Hartley showed Bulldogs as early as 1875. For a time he discontinued his work with the breed, but in 1892 he again began showing Bulldogs and exhibited until his death in 1905. Highwayman, Ace of Spades, Ida Nelson, Billy Nelson, and Rex Nelson were among the good specimens owned by Mr. Hartley.

Mr. W. T. Rylance owned the sound massive dog Lord Yarmouth, and two fine bitches, Lady Regent and Lady R. He also bred Conspirator, whelped in 1894, who was one of the best sons of Don

Solano. Conspirator, later owned by Mr. Sidney Swift, was shown extensively and was a consistent winner. Sina, Spice, and Orrel Mustard were other successful show dogs owned by Mr. Swift.

Mr. A. J. Sewell owned, Ch. Queer Street, and Mr. Mills had Ch. Heath Baronet, Ch. Uxbridge Matchless, and Uxbridge Marquis. Mr. Atkinson Jowett owned Ch. Pressgang, and two good bitches, Kentish Pride and Floradora.

In his first attempt at breeding, Mr. Geoffrey C. Swire bred Ch. Broadlea Squire, who was sold to Mr. J. W. Proctor, the owner of Ch. Kitty Royal, Mobberly Menestral, and Hematite, an excellent trio. Mr. Swire also bred the good dog Melampus.

Also prominent at the shows of the 1890's were Mr. H. A. Marfleet's Ch. Bromley Crib, and Mr. A. Fergusson's Swashbuckler, Ch. Moston Michael, Rory O'More, Sir Fergo, Blinkbonny, and The Scarlet Pimpernel. Mr. Charles Dark had Hazelmere Prince, a son of Prince Albert, and such other good specimens as Amber Duchess, Hazelmere Tom, and Hazelmere Countess. Among the exceptionally fine stock owned by Mr. Pegg (a well-known fancier who judged Bulldog shows both in England and the United States) were Champions Sally Lunn, Woodcote Chinosol, and Woodcote Bouncer. The excellent Chinosol, whelped in 1899 and bred by Mr. Chaundler, unfortunately died at the age of eighteen months. Had he lived long enough to be used extensively at stud, Chinosol would undoubtedly have had a good deal of influence on the breed, for he was an exceptionally sound, really good dog.

Although Mr. C. W. Brown was continually plagued with ill luck in his breeding operations, he owned and showed such good Bulldogs as Thackeray Primstone, Pamela, Duke of Cornwall, Torkington Model, Arbitratrix, and Doorkeeper.

Mr. R. G. S. Mann, owner of John of the Funnels, the famous progenitor of Ch. Rodney Stone and the Stone-bred dogs, owned an exceptionally good bitch in Liza Awkins. In addition to breeding and showing exceptional Bulldogs, Mr. Mann was a writer on the breed whose judicious opinions were carefully considered by other Bulldog breeders. Both Mr. Mann and Mr. A. M. Hodgson were staunch Bulldog men and through their work in the Bulldog Club, Incorporated, did much to further the interest in the Bulldog. Among Mr. Hodgson's dogs were Harper and Highwayman.

Mr. E. W. Jaquet, one-time secretary of the Kennel Club, owned a good specimen in Ayessha, sired by Don Pedro. Mr. F. W. Taylor entered the fancy as an exhibitor by purchasing the outstanding Ch. Baron Sedgemere, Ch. Battledora, and Hiarta. Mr. and Mrs. W. W. Crocker exhibited Lady Hamilton II, Hushmush, Ch. Buddug, and Traddles. In Mr. W. P. Kidd's kennel about that time were Willsid, Bobupanwyn, Hematite, and Magnetite.

Mr. J. W. Ross owned Tomsh and Ch. Blackwall Beauty, and Mr. F. O. Smith owned a good bitch, Bullet, sired by Rustic King ex Meg. Later, Mr. Smith bred Survivor, a massive specimen whelped in 1898, sired by Baron Stockwell ex Santissima. Mr. Armstrong, one of the early show enthusiasts of the Lancashire district, owned the good dog Bowdon Horatius, by Lord Yarmouth ex Hitcham Nettle.

Mr. Tom Mackness showed Fickle Fortune (whelped in 1898, by Fortunes Frolic ex Fugitive) and Fortunatus (whelped in 1900, by Fortunes Frolic ex Doctor Janet). Mr. H. C. Brucker, who bred Ace of Spades, also showed Battle Axe and the heavy-weight Baby Bacchus. Mr. C. Jemmet-Browne, a well-known writer for "Our Dogs," had some good winners in Bulwark, Ortersutem, and Bobupanwyn.

Under the Felton prefix, Mr. and Mrs. Marley had many good specimens, some of which were home-bred dogs. Among the very good ones they showed were Felton Duchess, Felton Prince, Felton Regent, Felton Comet, and Felton Earl. Mr. J. W. Hall, another successful breeder but one who kept only a small kennel, owned Lady Albertstone (a Prince Albert daughter), who was the dam of Lord Roundcroft. Unfortunately, the latter died just as he was making a big name as a stud. Dot Roundcroft and Regal Roundcroft were two of Mr. Hall's fine home-bred specimens. Others in Mr. Hall's kennels were Carbineer, Clansman, Coadjutor, and the good bitch Clairvoyant, an outstanding winner in 1907.

Mr. G. E. Hasleham showed Withington Rufus and Withington Consul. The former was bred by Mr. Sidney Deacon, an enthusiastic Bulldog fancier whose interest in the breed continued over a period of a great many years, and a man who did much to further the interest in the Bulldog through his writings as well as through his work with the clubs and at shows.

Mr. Edgar Farman, author of *The Bulldog* (1899) was the breeder of Felon, whelped in 1889, by Don Pedro ex Ophelia. During the latter days of their show careers, Ch. Ruling Passion, Ch. Cigarette, Rose, and Dan were owned by Mr. Farman. Captain

126

Ch. Samson Esquire (Golden Doubloon ex Lady of Bolton), owned by C. G. Heseltine.

Ch. Leodride Beau Son.

Beamish, who judged shows both in England and the United States, owned a most successful stud dog, Pleasant Bertie.

From as early as the 1890's, Mr. H. Schlaferman's Kilburn Kennels in London were among the better-known kennels. Mr. Schlaferman's first outstanding winners were Ch. His Lordship, Catseye, and Lordling, the latter a dog that did a great deal of winning during 1893 and 1894. Mr. Schlaferman was considered one of the very best Bulldog judges in England, and turned out a number of champions down through the years, as well as exporting many famous Bulldogs. Mr. Schlaferman's good dogs included Ch. Boaz, Ch. Kilburn Magnet, and Ch. Mahomet (all three of which were also shown under the ownership of other fanciers at some period during their careers). Among the famous dogs which Mr. Schlaferman exported were Ch. Mahomet, Ch. St. Vincent, Ch. Lord Chancellor, Ch. Parkhurst, Ch. Kilburn Magnet, Ch. Rockcliff Hats Off (first known as Kilburn Baby Boy), Kilburn Ring, Kilburn President, Kilburn Captain, Chepstow Scrooge, Ch. Bender, and Ch. Florence Bender. One of Mr. Schlaferman's outstanding stud dogs was Kilburn Regal, a consistent prize-winner, who has been described as one of England's most outstanding Bulldogs.

Mr. George Raper owned and bred many good dogs. Among them were Ch. Rustic King, Rustic Model, Rustic Hero, and Rustic Sovereign. One of the most famous of the dogs at Mr. Raper's kennels was Ivel Rustic (at one time known as Ivel Divel), who was bred by Mrs. C. B. Evans, by General Roberts ex Ivel Nana. Rabajas, who was bred by Mr. Raper, was exported to America but later was returned to England.

Mr. Charles G. Hopton bred many fine dogs, both in England and America. He was a gifted writer on the Bulldog and judged at many of the top shows in England and America. A host of good Bulldogs bore Mr. Hopton's Rodney prefix, including such outstanding specimens as Rodney Rosador, Rodney King, and Rodney Monarch. Mr. Hopton was also the breeder of L'Ambassadeur, the first American-bred champion.

Another of the greats of Bulldogdom was Sam Woodiwiss, a breeder who entered into a scientific program of breeding and at the height of his success stood practically alone at the top of the ladder. At one time Mr. Woodiwiss had in his own kennels four champion dogs of his own breeding—Ch. Boaz, Ch. Baron Sedgemere, Ch. Battledora, and Ch. Blackberry. In addition to the aforementioned

Ch. Morovian He's A Mainstay (Morovian Mainstay ex Jackath White Velvet). Photo courtesy of Mr. and Mrs. R. Dickens.

dogs, others of his grand lot were Ch. British Monarch, Ch. Dryad, Ch. Taurus, and Ch. Datholite. Mr. Woodiwiss paid the then record sum of one thousand two hundred fifty dollars for Dockleaf, a dog which at the time of the transaction had never been entered in a show. Dockleaf was first shown in 1892 and was a consistent winner, for he was a magnificent specimen. Among his many outstanding get was Ch. Homestead Lady Dockleaf, an exceptional bitch who possessed a grand head.

Mr. J. W. Kershaw, another of Britain's most successful breeders, owned Heywood Queen, an ideal brood bitch by Ch. Katerfelto. Heywood Queen was mated to Carthusian Cerberus twice, and produced Ch. Heywood Duchess, Hematite, and Magnetite. Ch. Heywood Duchess won her first challenge certificate at the age of ten months, and had acquired her championship title by the time she was seventeen months of age. An excellent show bitch, Ch. Heywood Duchess won seven challenge certificates before her death at the age of ten years. In addition to being an outstanding show winner, Ch. Heywood Duchess was an exceptional brood bitch, and the Heywood blood was much in demand. Among her progeny were twenty-two winners, and the prices obtained for puppies from Heywood Duchess were consistently high. Among her outstanding progeny were Ch. Kitty Royal, Ch. Silent Duchess, Ch. Heywood Beauty, Heywood Marquis, Heywood Victoria, Mobberley Menestral, Oneanonly, and Wilberdorf. Heywood Marquis was an exceptional specimen of the breed and made a great name as a stud dog.

Walter Jefferies is considered to be the most successful breeder of Bulldogs of modern times. For seven years he owned and bred Bulldogs but met with very little success. Then he produced Ch. Rodney Stone, and from that time on, his fame as a breeder was established. He introduced and perfected the Stone strain, and was one of the very first breeders to have a definite breeding program. He was also prominent in early Bulldog affairs. Among dogs he bred were True Type, Rival Stone, Dick Stone, and many others. Walter Jefferies, whose famous "Stone" prefix is world renowned, was the first breeder ever to sell a Bulldog for five thousand dollars. This dog, Rodney Stone, was sent to America to Richard Croker, Jr.

Regal Stone, another of Mr. Jefferies' famous dogs, was purchased by Mr. Buckler of Leicester, under whose ownership Regal Stone won his championship. Mr. Buckler, the first president of the Midland Radius Bulldog Club, did much to further the interests of the Bulldog.

The famous Roseville Kennels, presided over for a great many years by Mr. and Mrs. G. Woollons, produced Ch. Roseville Brilliant, Ch. Roseville Bystar, and Roseville Ban, among many other good ones. But the most outstanding Bulldog produced in this kennel was the illustrious Ch. Roseville Blaze, whelped on November 16, 1910, and one of the best Bulldog bitches ever produced. Mr. Woollons is another breeder who achieved a name for himself as an outstanding judge of the breed.

Mr. Luke Crabtree (mentioned previously) owned many exceptional Bulldogs—Ch. Boomerang, Ch. Katerfelto, Ch. Prince Albert, and Ch. Moston Michael, to name but a few. Mr. Crabtree bred Ch. Moston Roland, but this dog, while a good specimen, was not the equal of his famous sire, Ch. Prince Albert. Other Bulldogs sired by Prince Albert and numbered among the good dogs of the day were Ch. Broadlea Squire, Ch. Kitty Royal, Queen of Scots, Moston Consort, Prince of Darkness, Mobberley Menestral, and Hazelmere Prince. Mr. Crabtree's death was a great blow to the Bulldog fancy for he was not only an enthusiastic breeder, but was also active in Bulldog Club affairs for many years.

Sam Crabtree (a brother of Luke Crabtree) was a famous international Bulldog judge who judged at shows all over the world. Also an ardent fancier, Sam Crabtree was the owner of the famous Failsworth Kennels. One of his most outstanding Bulldogs, and probably his best, was Ch. Columba Rose, who was followed by Ch. Failsworth White Knight as a close second. Others from Mr. Crabtree's kennels were Ch. Failsworth White Marquis, Ch. Knight of Hollybrook, Ch. Failsworth White Orry, Failsworth Peggy, Failsworth Baron, and the famous Strathtay Prince Albert. The latter, bred by Colonel J. A. Edelston, and sold to Mr. Crabtree at the age of two years, was originally known as Norton Sambur. Since Strathtay Prince Albert gained his championship title in America, and also reached the zenith of his career there, he will be discussed at greater length in the chapter on American fanciers, shows and dogs.

James Kenworthy's kennels, also among the oldest and largest in Great Britain, housed one of England's greatest stud dogs, Chineham Joker, who was whelped on November 5, 1907. Chineham Joker mated with Colonel Edelston's Norton Violet produced

131

Strathtay Prince Albert (mentioned above) and a bitch puppy named Woodend Joan, who was an exceptional winner in 1913 and 1914 under the ownership of Mr. J. Whitehead. Since Chineham Joker was sired by Rival Stone ex Flower o' the Veldt, his progeny, which included a great many exceptionally fine Bulldogs, may be considered a branch of the famous Stone strain. On his dam's side, Chineham Joker was descended from Ch. Chineham Young Jack, for the latter was the sire of Flower o' the Veldt. Ch. Chineham Young Jack and Ch. Chineham Paradox were two exceptional specimens owned by Mr. Cannon, a well-known Bulldog judge.

The Mackworth Kennels of Mr. Stanley B. Jones at one time housed Mackworth Baroness and Ch. Woodend Joan, who competed and won in brace classes time after time. This kennel, located in Cardiff, was one of the oldest that exhibited at shows regularly.

Another kennel well-known in 1914 was Mr. Gerald Wellesley's Manor House Kennels, whose "Manor House" prefix appeared in the names of a number of good Bulldogs. Among his breeding stock were Manor House Milkmaid (a bitch twice inbred to Rodney Stone), Manor House Mistress, Manor House Merrythought and

English and American Ch. Juneter's Ace (Ch. Superb of Wiggin ex Juneter's Surprise), owned by Mrs. Gladys Creasey.

132

Manor House Mystery (a bitch twice inbred to Ch. Prince Albert).

Mr. Sydney Clifford's Chepstow Kennels produced prize-winners such as Lodden Chepstow Smiler, exported to Australia; Robinswood Scrooge (originally Chepstow Scrooge;, who was exported to America; Chepstow Sykes; Chepstow Squeers; Chepstow Lady Babs; Chepstow Mars; and the noted Fitz-Bosh. Chepstow Stell, whelped in 1912, by Carslake Rex ex Chepstow Lady Babs, was considered by many to be the pick of the kennel.

About that same time, the Cintra Kennels, belonging to Mr. A. W. Stallard, produced Cintra Helen, Cintra John, and Cintra Sarah, the latter a bitch who made phenomenal wins even at an early age.

Mr. Claude Bridgeland's kennels produced a number of good Bulldogs, including the famous bitch Ch. Totora. Another Bulldog bred by Mr. Bridgeland in 1910 was Stockwell Baronet, litter brother of Champions Lord Wealdstone, Maybank Minor, and Woodcote Hermit, and the sire of Ch. Amherst Baron and Ch. Stockwell Mayor.

Mr. Skidmore, of Buxton, the breeder of King of the Peak, was the owner of Peaceable and Buxtonia, the former being the sire of Champions Yamamoto and Phul Nanabred. The two last-named Bulldogs, bred by Mr. McPherson, enjoyed successful show careers. And Mrs. Proffitt had in her kennel Uxbridge Mauritania, Little John, Clinker Jack, and Flying Colours, all of whom had been shown successfully.

Mr. and Mrs. A. G. Sturgeon's kennel housed the beautiful Ch. Oak Nana, Oak Leaf, Destiny, Daggers Drawn, and Ch. Dame Daggers, as well as the outstanding bitch Ch. Dames Double, who won a record number of challenge certificates for a bitch. Ch. Oak Nana was considered the best Bulldog (either dog or bitch) exported to the United States up to that time. She was by Oak Leaf (by Solid Oak) and bred from a bitch who had no pretensions to show form but was obviously a bitch of quality.

During World War I, Bulldog breeding activities became somewhat subdued, but those breeders who were well established continued their breeding activities, though on a somewhat curtailed basis. And although some breeders were forced to discontinue their activities altogether, never to resume them, once the war was over, new fanciers entered the field so Bulldog breeding continued to flourish in Great Britain.

The Naylor brothers owned a Scotch-bred puppy named Yarrow-side Bangup (by Ch. Lochaber ex Seamew), which they later re-named Dunscar Draftsman. This dog, whelped in 1922, was a light fawn heavy-weight and acquired the title of champion. His chief fault was his ear carriage, but he was a great sire and proved himself by producing eleven champions. He is considered one of the great stud dogs of the century and among his get were Ch. Son O'Jill, Ch. Boltonia Barrister, Ch. Anglezarke Sheesadraftsman, Ch. Angle-zarke Sonny Boy, Ch. Mountain Lassie, Ch. Mountain Queen, Ch. Allithorne Rival, Ch. Crew So Solarium, Ch. Tweedside Red Chief, Ch. Carissima, Ch. Moizette, and Am. Ch. Dunscar Doctor. Ch. Dunscar Draftsman showed his prepotency at an early age and trans-mitted his quality bone and substance to his many descendants. Many good specimens were produced by crossing the blood of Ch. Dunscar Draftsman and Irish Alaunt. Mr. and Mrs. J. Berry owned Ch. Carissima, who obtained her championship title when about twelve months old. Unfortunately, this outstanding bitch died at a comparatively young age.

Mr. Cumberlidge, who owned Ch. Son O'Jill, and bred Ch. Bol-tonia Barrister, had three other champions: Ch. Springvale Silent Betty, Ch. Silent Jill, and Ch. Sunbarry.

Mr. and Mrs. Dinsley Cooper were the owners of the great stud dog Irish Alaunt, who, after winning a challenge certificate at the show of the Bulldog Club, Inc., and a reserve at Crufts, was retired from exhibition life. Among the get of Irish Alaunt were Ch. Wenden Citizen, Ch. Fancy Girl, Ch. Tufnell Launtett, Ch. Justso Jill, Ch. Pen-Y-Lan Duchess, Ch. Valiant Winnie, Am. Ch. Alaunt's Double, Am. Ch. Memento, and others. Irish Alaunt, by Tintagel ex Irish Lady Sam, was a very fine dog for the most part, though ropey in wrinkles and with rather thick ears. However, Irish Alaunt was a good sire and transmitted many of his good points to his progeny; unfortunately, he also passed on his heavy ears. Mr. and Mrs. Cooper also owned Irish Challenger, a Dudley, who was one of the outstanding progeny resulting from the combination of Prince Albert and Stone blood, and in his time sired some really good ones.

Ch. Tottonian Monarch, owned by Mr. M. C. Wright, caused a sensation at the 1926 show of the Bulldog Club, Inc., when he won the challenge certificate at eight months of age.

Following 1926, Ch. Pugilist was the outstanding winner for sev-

English and American Ch. Duranside Roddie.

Ch. Basford Ideal.

eral years, collecting thirty challenge certificates for his owner, Mrs. J. Walz. Pugilist was defeated once by the famous Ch. Anglezarke Sheesadraftsman, who had been acquired by Ernest Roddy.

Between World Wars I and II, Mr. Roddy set a record by producing three champions in one litter: Ch. Basford Gem, Ch. Basford Ideal, and Ch. Basford Elite. Mr. Roddy has owned and made more champions than any other man in the history of the breed. He campaigned twenty-three dogs to championship status—eight of which were home-bred. Ten of these twenty-three champions became tri-international champions. Also, Mr. Roddy exported five other Bulldogs that became champions after leaving England. Among the better known of Mr. Roddy's exports were Ch. Basford Ideal, Int. Ch. Basford Revival's Replica, Tri-Int. Ch. Basford Model, Ch. Basford Duranside Roddy, Ch. Basford Golden Nymph, Ch. Basford Vulconian Revenge, and Ch. Basford Shesabasford.

135

Mrs. Ivy Palmer, who had shown the bitch Ch. Cloverley Bitte several years before, returned to the show ring with the successful Cloverley Brunette, Ch. Cloverley Bachelor, Ch. Cloverley Benedict, and Ch. Cloverley Brightstar, as well as others.

The Glendene Kennels, owned by Mr. and Mrs. J. M. Taylor, housed the grand bitch Ch. Glendene Sunya, bred by Mrs. E. Johnson, who also bred Int. Ch. Jasperdin of Din, among other big winners.

Dr. Wm. Anderson's Muiravonside Kennels produced many fine Bulldogs. Among those that should be mentioned are Ch. Lochaber, Ch. Muiravonside Success, Ch. Donachadh Ban, Ch. Muiravonside Queen, Ch. Muiravonside Lass, Ch. Melisande, and Ch. Muiravonside Challenger, who was exported to America where he had an exceptionally successful career.

Mrs. L. D. Nichols' "Hefty" dogs are also among the outstanding Bulldogs produced in England. Among those she has had are Ch. Hefty Son of Mike, Ch. Hefty Master Grumpy, Ch. Hefty Barbara, Hefty Patricia, and Hefty Dauntless.

Mrs. Surtees Monkland, another successful breeder, owned Montem Susie, a bitch she mated to Ch. Challenger, producing a litter including Ch. Sweet September and Ch. All's Well. Others owned by Mrs. Monkland included Ch. Tintagel, Fair Isle, The Jabberwock, Cloth of Gold, and Golden Legend.

Mr. W. H. Taylor, who served as an officer in the British Bulldog Club, owned such good ones as Ch. Boltonia Barrister, Boltonia Bulwark, and Boltonia Bliss.

Mr. and Mrs. Carlo F. C. Clarke must be included as ardent fanciers of the breed. Mrs. Clarke's "Mersham" prefix is well-known and among the best Bulldogs exhibited by her are Mersham Charmer, Beautiful Benjamin, Mersham Soda, Mersham Hetty, Mersham Ham, and Mersham Shem.

Mr. James Leeming's kennel has housed Ch. Crewe So Glenalmond, Ch. Crewe So Mignonette, Ch. Tweedside Red Chief, Ch. Crewe So Solarium, and Ch. Crewe So Viceregal.

Among the well-known winners exhibited by Mr. and Mrs. Hubert Wright are Vindex Vizor, Ch. Vindex Versa, Ch. Clarinda, Ch. Vindex Vistar, and Marigold.

Mr. J. M. Knight's successful kennel included a very sound bitch, Ch. Hainault Duchess. Mr. F. W. Crowther owned the good dog

136

Ch. Koper Kernel (Flisctonian Bomber ex Golden Ballerina), was an English champion and the sire of the renowned Ch. Kippax Fearnought.

Enfield Grabber and the bitch Enfield Tarlet, as well as others.

A few fanciers kept their kennels active during the very trying times that came with World War II. Among those who carried on were Mrs. Reid, Mr. and Mrs. Woollons, John Barnard, Taylor, Edwards, Roddy, Asplin, Allen, and Mrs. Smith. Mr. and Mrs. S. H. Smith, of "Grenville" fame, exported a number of dogs and are justly proud of their Grenville Bashington. Mrs. Smith is a championship show judge and has judged in the United States. Mr. A. Brooks' "Duranside" prefix is another to be found among the names of winning Bulldogs.

Of the dogs bred during the World War II years, the two greatest that continued on afterwards were Allithorne Resolution and Peter Beautiful. The Allithorne Kennels, owned by Mr. and Mrs. A. C. Asplin, had previously produced other outstanding Bulldogs, the most notable perhaps being Allithorne Rival. Bred by W. J. Edwards, Allithorne Resolution ex Maelor Veronica produced the litter whelped October 14, 1945, containing three champions; Ch. Maelor Solarium, Ch. Maelor Uplifter, and Ch. Beautiful Bunty.

It is impossible to overestimate the influence which these litter

Ch. Maelor Solarium.

Ch. Maelor Invincible.

Ch. Maelor Superb.

Peter Beautiful.

brothers, particularly Solarium, had on the breed during the immediate post-war period. Their progeny were noted for their remarkable, fine heads and superb underjaws. There are few present-day dogs who can not trace at least one line back to one of these great sires. Ch. Maelor Solarium tied Ch. Dunscar Draftsman's record by siring eleven English champions; Ch. Ritestok Robin Hood, Ch. Superb of Wiggin, Ch. Greenville Bashington, Ch. Brownslane Buddy, Ch. Holcombe View Nancy, Ch. Greenville Gay Queen, Ch. Pelsallette, Ch. Maelor Superb, Ch. Maelor Invincible, Ch. Milord of the Regions, Ch. Ultima Cleopatra and Am. Ch. Whiskehob Lord Calvert.

Ch. Maelor Uplifter sired seven English champions: Ch. Roseville Brightglare, Ch. Cheetham's Pride, Ch. Paddy's Dawn, Ch. Belwood Buccaneer, Ch. Jonsah Success, Ch. Eastgate Demirep of Craggvale and Ch. Drewan Daphne. He died comparitvely young in 1950 or his total might have matched his brother's. The list of their other winners in England and overseas is endless. Perhaps someone, somewhere, will have the good fortune to breed, in the near future, a dog which can match the achievements of Ch. Maelor Solarium, and stamp his image on the Bulldogs of the future.

Peter Beautiful, a dog with a grand head, was three times inbred to Ch. Obstinate Artist (a dog who also had a fine skull, but was a poor mover). In Peter Beautiful, the triple cross of this champion progenitor was at times reflected by the lack of perfection in hocks and stifles apparent in some of his get.

At this time Mr. and Mrs. John Barnard's great Ch. Prince of Woodgate has equaled the records of Ch. Dunscar Draftsman and Ch. Maelor Solarium and has sired eleven English champions. I wonder who will be the great to sire twelve champions and a new all-time record.

The Morovian Bulldog Kennels are widely known both in England and America. Owned by Mr. H. C. Horsefield, this kennel made Bulldog history with the great stud dog Morovian Mainstay, the sire of many good dogs both in England and America, including Am. Ch. Morovian He's A Mainstay. Mainstay was bred by Mr. and Mrs. Prophet of Manchester, and was a litter-brother of Falstone Sensation. Mr. B. R. Sharpe, who established his Falstone Bulldog Kennels in 1899 bred and exported many good dogs. Among them were Int. Ch. Falstone Duchess and Am. Ch. Falstone Sensation, who was the sire of Am. Ch. Elvinar's Falstone Torpedo.

139

Ch. Walvra Red Ensign owned by Mr. N. Pitts and bred by Mrs. V. May.

Ch. Prince of Woodgate (Ch. Dunvegan Falstone Rodney ex Wynne of
Woodgate), owned by John Barnard.

Morovian Mainstay (Peter Beautiful
ex Ameswaite Pal O'Sunshine). Photo
courtesy of H. C. Horsefield.

Allithorne Renown, owned
by Allithorne Kennels.

Mr. John Barnard and his "Noways" Bulldogs have been very popular. Some of the better known Bulldogs produced by his kennel were Ch. Noways Cherry, Ch. Noways Timber and Ch. Noways Chuckles, the first Bulldog bitch to go best in show at Crufts, the largest dog show in the world. This outstanding bitch made the phenomenal 1952 win in an entry of over six thousand dogs.

Mr. and Mrs. A. E. Smith were experienced Bulldog breeders and both championship show judges. Also Mr. Smith was a qualified writer on the breed. Among the many good ones whose names include the "Leodride" prefix of the Smiths' was Ch. Leodride Beau Son, regarded as an exceptionally good specimen. Another postwar fancier who had outstanding success is H. D. Clayton (Wiggin), whose dogs include Ch. Superb of Wiggin, Eng. and Am. Ch. Red Roger of Wiggin, Ch. Amrondines Rockafella of Wiggin, and Am. Ch. Red Boomerang of Wiggin.

Mrs. Hope van Raalte (Hollycroft Kennels) purchased from Mr. Frank Thompson the bitch Ch. Hollycroft Sunday, and from Miss Whitehead the bitch Ch. Hollycroft Sugar.

Other breeders and kennels whose names should be mentioned are Jimmie Allen (Altonian); H. Dooler (Kippax); L. Cotton (Aldridge); Mr. and Mrs. N. Pitts (Allomdom); Mr. and Mrs. R. H. W. Black (Annadic); A. Dryden Stuart (Ardryen); E. Kenyon (Atomstone); Mr. and Mrs. J. Goodacre (Bannerjee); Mr. and Mrs. V. C. Haynes (Barranco); Mr. and Miss Bowers (Bowcrest); Mr. and Mrs. A. T. Laker (Bullculler); Mr. R. N. Chambers (Castizo); Mr. and Mrs. A. Smith (Damefoldo); Mr. and Mrs. John Davies (Dewrie); Mr. E. Jamieson (Ellivesor); Mrs. M. M. L. Cook (Eskaidee); Mr. and Mrs. J. Story (Minotaur); Mrs. Marjorie Barnard (Noways); Mrs. D. Wakefield (Outdoors); Mrs. S. Goddard (Portfield); Mr. L. Lund (Qualco); Mr. and Mrs. A. F. Saunders (Sevenup); Mrs. D. Thorpe (Tuffnuts); Jack Cook and Mr. and Mrs. W. J. Lawlor (Rockliffe).

Among top-flight Bulldogs not previously mentioned are Ch. Bellwood Buccaneer, Ch. John Blockbuster, Ch. Cheetham's Pride, Ch. Paddy's Dawn, Ch. Koper Kernal, Ch. Noway's Bodie, Eng. and Am. Ch. Jackath Silver Cloud, Eng. and Am. Ch. Banshee of Beechlyn, Eng. and Am. Ch. Eastgate Stalwart Bosum, Am. Ch. Beau Paradise Ideal, Eng. Ch. Drewand Daphne, Eng. and Am. Ch. Threethorne Honeylight of Ashford, Eng. and Am. Ch. Altonian Snowstorm

Ch. Noways Cherry (Ch. Prince of Woodgate ex Noways Victoria), owned by John Barnard.

Ch. Noways Chuckles.

Ch. Noways Timber (Ch. Prince of Woodgate ex Noways Victoria) bred by J. Barnard, Jr.

Several Bulldog toppers of the 1970's in England are Ch. Rockliffe's Thydeal Audacious; Ch. Kalbirchan Lord Percy; Ch. Bellum Premiere, 1977 Bulldog of the Year; Ch. Aldridge Anemone, Top Bulldog 1978; Ch. Outdoors Jubilant, 1978 Bulldog of the Year; Ch. Aldridge Advent Gold; Ch. Jackath Stargazer and Ch. Soldier Boy of the Regions.

O'Vardona, Eng. and Am. Ch. Marquis of the Hills, Eng. and Am. Ch. Duranside Roddy, Eng. and Am. Ch. Kippax Fearnought and his litter brother Eng. and Am. Ch. Kippax Dreadnought, Eng. and Am. Ch. Juneter's Ace, Am. Ch. Brindle Duchess, Eng. and Am. Ch. Altonian Supermist, Ch. Bradford Foden Esquire, Am. Ch. Overfen Faith, Eng. and Am. Ch. Overfen Helen, Ch. Baytor Bosun, Ch. Baytor Greathill Bunty, Ch. Threethorne Honeylight, Ch. Noways Sunrise, Ch. Thydeal Relentless, Ch. Baytor Archilles of Cinric, Ch. Denbrough Leander, Ch. Allomdom Dilkusha Crusader, Ch. Ellesmere Duchess, Dewrie Drummer Boy, and Ch. Daneham Cinderella—all a representative group to be proud of.

Closely related to the English foundation stock are the following outstanding dogs that represent modern strains in America: Ch. Cockney Gorblimey, Ch. Elvinar's Falstone Torpedo, Ch. Dour Dispatch, Ch. Morovian Stormer's Draftsman, Ch. Dicken's Newlo's Golden Nymph, Ch. Hanes' Little May, Ch. Draftsman's Choice O'Vardona, Ch. Maxmal Climax, Ch. Wixey, Ch. Michael Pendergast, Ch. O'Sandy Jiggs II, Ch. Mapo's Sandman, Ch. Vardona Frosty Snowman, Ch. Vardona Snowman's Double, Ch. Ashford Sandstone, Ch. Marmac's Bold Venture, Ch. Shadow's Smasher, Ch. Hetherbull's Arrogance, Ch. Vardona's Frosty Masterpiece, Ch. Bayside Doubloon, Ch. Min-A Sota Fats of Kelley Road, and a host of others who, for lack of space, will have to be omitted.

Top Bulldogs exported in the last few years are Ch. Jackath Silver Cloud, Ch. Blackshots Captain Cook, Ch. Tuffnuts First Lady, Ch. Qualco Marksman, Ch. Thydeal Relentless, Can. and Am. Ch. Harada Bashington, Am. Ch. Blackshots Ivanhoe and Am. Ch. Big Ben of Essex to the United States; Ch. Toby Jug of Wyngrove to Japan and Ch. Crossroads Calphurnia to Switzerland.

The top English sire in the 1960's was Tredgold Gaius Caligula, a grandson of Ch. Maelor Solarium, who was bred by Mr. N. Gladstone and owned by Mr. I. Sidgwick. Caligula was a very handsome dog with heavy bone and a great head. He never became a cham-

English and American Ch. Jackath Silver Cloud, owned by Dickensbrae Kennels. This bitch became a top winner in the breed and a multiple group and Best in Show winner in America.

Ch. Lamerit Cornflower of Wyngrove, bred by Mr. J. J. Harrison.

Tredgold G a i u s Caligula

Ch. Thydeal Relentless

Ch. Tuffnuts First Lady

pion because of displays of temperament in the ring. He sired a great many champions including Ch. Albermar Beefeater, Ch. Albermar Bonanza and Ch. Scarlet O'Hara, all in one litter. Ch. Qualco Marksman, Ch. Baron of Blythome, Ch. Belnan Chieftain, Ch. Goulceby Craigatin Brave Boy and Ch. Ritestok Toprilt Paul of Tarsus.

Some of the good ones that remained at home and were never exported are: Ch. Thydeal Little Audie, Ch. Lamerit Cornflower of Wyngrove, Ch. Baytor Telstar, Ch. Bryneatons Bikini, Ch. Outdoors Kippand, Ch. Outdoors Boozer, Ch. Mellea Hesagenie, Ch. Walvra Sans Souci, Ch. Baytor Bosun, Ch. Walvra Red Ensign, Ch. Broomwick Barrister, Ch. Albermar Beefeater, Ch. Albermar Bonanza, Ch. Scarlet O'Hara, Ch. Blockbuster Best Bitter, Ch. Belnan Chieftain, Ch. Castizo Drummond, Ch. Broomwick Blythome Bumble Bee, Ch. Auralean Activator and Ch. Fairtrough Louis.

Ch. Lamerit Cornflower of Wyngrove was the winner of 15 C.C.'s, one Irish Green Star, 112 Best in Shows and 320 First Prizes, Specialty and All-Breed shows under fifteen different judges. Her breeder was J. J. Harrison. Ch. Walvra Red Ensign was Best of Breed at Crufts two years running and Ch. Thydeal Little Audie won 15 Challenge Certificates. Her strongest point was probably her truly great head.

The breed is now experiencing a revival in England and registrations are now exceeding 1,000 per year. The Bulldog Club, Inc. is as strong as ever and its annual championship show is the largest Bulldog event of the year. The Club celebrated its centenary in 1975 with one of the greatest shows of all times. The Bulldog Club, Inc. is the oldest breed club in the world and 1980 marks the anniversary of Marjorie Barnard's 21st year as President of the British parent body.

It might be well to note that the Standard adopted in May 1875 by The Bulldog Club, remains the same as originally adopted, except for the weight being raised from 50 pounds to 55 pounds in the 1950's.

Ch. Rawburn Gleneagles, owned by Dorothy R. Trammelle.

American Fanciers, Dogs
and Shows

T HE first Bulldog in America of which we have record was Donald, exhibited by Sir William Verner at the 1880 show in New York. By Alpha ex Vixen, Donald was whelped in 1875 and at maturity weighed about forty pounds. He was a brindle and white dog with a good head, but he was not too commendable in other respects.

According to the records of The American Kennel Club, the first Bulldog to attain his championship status in America was Robinson Crusoe, who became a champion in 1888. C. G. Hopton, with his Ch. L'Ambassadeur, was the first man in America to breed an American champion.

In 1881 Charles H. Mason brought out two dogs, Ch. Alexander and Noble, both of whom were considered superior to Donald. A fairly frequent winner in England, the latter was winner in the 1881 New York show where Bonnie Boy, sired by the English dog Slenderman and owned by Mr. John P. Barnard, placed second.

About this same time, Mr. James Mortimer owned the good dog

White Knight of Anoakia

Ch. Knight Errant of Anoakia at 14 months. He was the winner of the Non-Sporting group at the Westminster Kennel Club in 1920.

Blister, which he later sold to Colonel John E. Thayer. Colonel Thayer was the breeder of Guillermo (an outstanding winner in 1885), and the importer of the litter-mates Ch. Robinson Crusoe and Ch. Britomartis (sired by Ch. Monarch ex Penzie, and whelped in July 1881). These two imported dogs were without doubt the two best specimens of the breed exhibited in the United States up to that time, and Britomartis placed first at the New York shows from 1885 until 1890.

Mr R Livingston appeared next with his Ch. Boz, by Gamester; Bellona, a daughter of Mr. Harry Layton's Warwick; and Panther, a young son of Ch. Sancho Panza. Trenor L. Park, the first Vice-President of the Bulldog Club of America, imported Gipsy King, by Alaric; Dimple, a daughter of Oswego; Ch. Bedgebury Lion, a brindle-pied who had a sensational show record in England; Lena Langtry; and Monarch IV.

Mr. A. F. Nash, of Chicago, imported the good bitch Dolores, a brindle by Grabber ex Donna Sol, and a winner at the English Bulldog Club shows in 1886 and 1887. Mr. E. A. Woodward, also of Chicago, was for some years secretary of the Bulldog Club of America and an ardent promoter of the breed. He imported Charmion; Bo's-wain; Cleopatra; Lady Nan (a good bitch by Harper and the one from which Mr. Woodward bred Argonaut, one of the good early American-bred Bulldogs); Princess Crib, a daughter of Reeve's Crib; Ch. King Lud, the son of Ch. Pathfinder; Peckham Lass, by Sir Garnet Wolseley; Duchess of Parma, a daughter of Ch. British Monarch; and other good ones.

It is to the Bulldogs mentioned in the foregoing paragraphs that many of the best American strains owe their origin.

A fancier of the later eighties was Mr. H. D. Kendall, of Lowell, Massachusetts, whose kennel stock included the white dog Bathos (bred by Mr. C. F. W. Jackson); Dolly Tester, a winning daughter of Black Prince; and Portswood Tiger, a heavy-weight who became a champion.

Although Bulldogs had been imported and shown in this country since 1880; prior to 1890 there was no organized club by fanciers of the breed. In 1890, H. D. Kendall conceived the idea of forming an organization to "join together for the purpose of encouraging the thoughtful and careful breeding of the English Bulldog in America, to perpetuate the purity of the strain, to improve the quality of

151

native stock, and to remove the undesirable prejudice that existed in the public mind against a most admirable breed." He called together all interested fanciers at Mechanics Hall in Boston on April 1, 1890 to form what today is the Bulldog Club of America.

The Standard used by the English Bulldog Club was adopted as the American Standard. However exhibitors felt that this standard was not concise enough, so in 1894 a committee was formed to develop an American Standard. After much study the committee presented their recommendations to the membership and the Standard as we know it today, with a few modifications, was adopted. Soon after the formation of the club, Mr. R. B. Sawyer imported a good trio: Harper (a son of Ch. British Monarch), and two bitches, Graven Image and Holy Terror. All three had made good show records in England.

Mr. E. D. Morgan appeared next with his "Wheatley" team comprised of Ch. Pathfinder; Ch. Saleni (said to have been the best bitch seen in America up to that time); Cardinal Wolseley; and Carrie a daughter of British Monarch.

Mr. E. K. Austin imported several Bulldogs, including Sheriff, a red-hearted brindle dog which died soon after landing; Princess Venn, an extremely low fawn and white bitch by Don Salano; and Baron Killarney, a son of Smartt's Punch. Mr. Charles D. Cugle, of Baltimore, owned Bombardos, a fawn and white dog by British Monarch; Derby Hebe and Derby Nance, two good bitches by Reeve's Crib; and Skipper, a son of Black Prince. Mr. John H. Matthews' kennel at this time included the white dog Bathos and the bitch Rose.

Among the breeders of prominence in the early nineties was Mr. J. P. Barnard, who bred Jack Horner, a winning son of King Cole, Jr.; Mr. Frank F. Dole, who produced the winners Lord Sheffield, Blount, Norfolk Swell, and Edgewood Mab; Mr. Sam Green, who bred Heathen II (by Heathen ex Magpie II); Mr. W. B. North, who bred Handsome Dan, probably the best American-bred up to that time and a dog which had the distinction of being the Yale mascot; Mr. E. Sheffield Porter; and Mr. John Cole.

Mr. Carl Haggenjos was another American fancier who bred and exhibited Bulldogs. His first winner was Jack Spratt (by Rabagas ex Nino), and he also owned a bitch by King Lud. In 1893 Mr. Haggenjos purchased Ch. Bo'swain from Mr. E. A. Woodward. This dog

Ch. Zorro Torro Lujo. Photo courtesy of E. S. Windfield.

Ch. Sandow, owned by Mrs. A. R. Glass.

Ch. Nugget My Ideal.

was one of the famous litter that included the two champion bitches Saleni and Ruling Passion. Among the dogs imported by Mr. Haggenjos were Woodcote Orry and Woodcote Don (purchased from Mr. Pegg); Yeovil Lion; Clyde Nestor; Prince Royal; Royal Rouge; Earl of Egmont; and Uxbridge Melayr. All of these, with the exception of Royal Rouge, were well-known winners in England. Rodney President, Silas Marner, and Rodney Coronation were among the dogs purchased by Mr. Haggenjos in America. The good ones bred by Mr. Haggenjos included Bill Junior, a winner in 1897, and Houri II, winner of a number of first and second prizes at prominent shows and also the winner of the Bulldog Club Medal in 1901. The much discussed Brutus Royal, a son of Prince Royal, was also bred by Mr. Haggenjos.

Mr. R. B. Sawyer's good dog Harper was shown by Mr. F. W. Sackett in 1891 and won the Parke Challenge Cup from Merry Monarch. Handsome Dan, the Yale Bulldog, was a winner in the novice class that year, and the following year won third in the open class.

In 1892 the Bulldog Club obtained a much fuller classification and a division by weight, and forty dogs were entered in the show. Mr. Woodward's kennel, which had been prominent at Canadian shows in 1892 with Bo'swain, won the challenge class prize, but was beaten by the bitch Saleni for the Parke Cup, and by King Lud in competition for Best of Opposite Sex.

Entries at the 1893 New York show indicated an increase of fifty percent over the total entries for the previous year, and there seemed no doubt that the Bulldog was well established in America. At this time Harper returned to his position at the head of the challenge class, but in competition for the cup was beaten by Leonidas, who won in the open class for Bulldogs over forty-five pounds. King Lud also won over Harper for one of the specials.

An importation of note in 1893 was Mr. Traver's Ch. His Lordship; then Damon, a cobby brindle by Ch. Datholite, was brought over; and Reve-Royal, Cameron, and Lady Monarch were imported by Charles G. Hopton. Also in 1893, James Mortimer brought over Ch. King Orry for Colonel Hilton. King Orry was for the most part white with very dark (also black) markings, and the importation of this famous dog, noted for his excellent head, had a decided effect on the breeding programs already established in America.

154

Dickens' Turoca Fonzi Jake, owned by Dickensbrae Kennels.

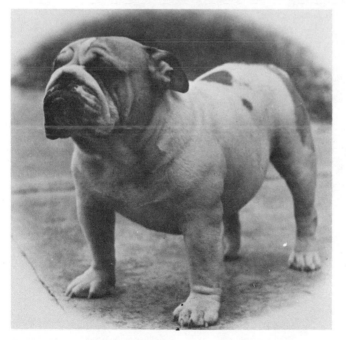

Ch. Kyleken Ferdinand The Bull, owned by Kyleken Kennels.

Ch. Murray's Mac Kac (Ch. Rich Pilgrim Beans ex Princess of Battles), owned by Ruth Emert.

Ch. Ideal of Maple Lodge.

Now that the breed was being represented strongly in the shows, several American-bred Bulldogs of promise appeared. Among them were Counsellor, Cock Robin, Rustic King II, Primrose, and Nobby Twist.

At the New York show in the spring of 1894, Mr. E. A. Woodward judged and placed His Lordship first; King Lud second; and King Orry third. The following year Colonel Hilton imported Ch. Facey Romford (a brindle and white dog by King Orry), who had a phenomenal career for one season, then died leaving none of his stock behind.

In 1896 Mr. Hopton's L'Ambassadeur won over Handsome Dan for the Field Cup. That same year, Mr. Tyler Morse and Mr. Bulkley Wells, both from Boston, entered the Bulldog fancy. Mr. Morse imported Rustic Sultan (who became known to American fanciers as Beaver Brook Sultan); Beaver Brook Empress, a brindle bitch with an excellent head; Rustic Phenomenon, perhaps the heaviest dog shown to that date in America; and other good ones. Mr. Wells' kennel included Lord Yarmouth, Jenny Jones, Fortunio, and other outstanding Bulldogs. At that time, Mr. Hopton's Rodney Kennels housed the famous Bulldogs Lady Monarch, Rodney Pelagia, the excellent Rodney Merlin (all three of which made exceptional show records), and of course the famous Ch. L'Ambassadeur.

About 1896, the Don Salano strain, which invariably produced low cobby specimens, became as popular in America as it was in England. Among dogs of this strain listed among the winners in the late nineties were Dandy Venn, his brother Orient Don, and Pleasant (imported in 1897 by Mr. J. H. Mullins). Other good dogs imported in 1897 were Pressmoor Force (afterwards known as Rodney); His Lordship; Don Juan; Ladas; Baron Stockwell; Orleston Toddlekins (known in America as Glenwood Queen); and Silver King. The latter two were shown by Mr. William C. Codman in the autumn of 1897 when he made his first appearance as an exhibitor in the United States. That same year, Lord Yarmouth won the Grand Trophy for best of breed at the New York show.

The New York show of 1898 showed a radical change from the entry of three years before. The classification had been changed, and the duplication of entries produced well-filled classes. There were forty-seven entries in five dog classes; fifty-one bitches in the corresponding classes for that sex; and four entries in a mixed sex class

157

for Bulldogs under twenty-five pounds. Mr. Woodward judged, placing Mr. Russell A. Alger's Rensal Dandy Venn over everything, including Orient Don in the novice and junior classes. Since Mr. Alger was not a member of the Bulldog club, Orient Don won the Challenge Cup, defeating the best bitch, Glenwood Queen, and Pleasant was third. The placing of the winners caused some controversy, and when Pleasant and Dandy Venn met on three occasions later that year, positions were reversed with Pleasant first in the winners classes.

When Mr. Raper came from England to judge the 1899 New York show, he brought Ivel Rustic with him. This truly exceptional Bulldog won first in winners classes at every show in which he was entered that year.

About that time, Mr. Joseph B. Vandergrift became interested in Bulldogs and he and Mr. Richard Croker, Jr., who was just entering the fancy, set a pace in exhibiting that was difficult for other fanciers to equal. Among Mr. Vandergrift's first purchases for his Vancroft Kennels were King Solomon, Orient Don, and Mersham Jock. Then he purchased Katerfelto (who was a son of King Orry and became one of Mr. Vandergrift's top dogs), Homestead Lady Dockleaf, Housewife, Marita, Yorkshire Relish, and the exceptional heavy-weight, Portland. Mr. Vandergrift's dogs were placed at stud at a very reasonable fee, with the consequence that a good crop of youngsters appeared sired by Mersham Jock, Rodney Grabber, and others.

Mr. Croker created quite a sensation by his purchase in England of the fabulous Ch. Rodney Stone from Walter Jefferies for five thousand dollars, the greatest sum ever paid for a Bulldog up to that time. Ch. Rodney Stone was a good all-round dog, a dark brindle with white chest and short legs which were muscular and not bowed, with plenty of bone and substance, nicely rounded ribs and sound hindquarters. He was a dog with a well-defined muzzle, great depth of face and lay-back, and his ears were very nicely placed, though perhaps too large, but certainly of the correct rose type and well carried. Another of Mr. Croker's good imports was Ch. Bromley Crib, a dog which weighed forty-five pounds, and for which he reportedly paid another high figure—four thousand dollars. He also imported Ch. Petramosse, Ch. Persimmon, Bit of Bluff, Little Witch, and others.

Sea Breeze Carl, owned by R. L. Dickens.

Smith's Sir Charles Chaplyn, owned by Kathy Smith.

Glenwood Queen (later a champion) won the Grand Trophy for Best of Breed in 1899 and 1900, the latter year winning over Persimmon and Petramosse. Purchased by George S. Thomas from Mrs. Evans, Ch. Ivel Doctor appeared next and won all over the country, winning the special for best of all breeds on many occasions.

For his Dreamwold Kennels, Mr. Thomas Lawson purchased the fawn dog Fashion, Ch. Ivel Monarch, Rodney Monarch, Thackeray Soda, Ch. Glenn Monarch, Ch. General Donax, and Ch. La Roche, a bitch for which Mr. Lawson paid six thousand dollars.

Dr. Henry D. Coghlan, of Chicago, was another American breeder of the early twentieth century. Baby Bullet, The Nipper and Captain Jinks represented his breeding stock as far as stud dogs were concerned. Among the bitches at Mr. Coghlan's kennel at Dorchester Farm in Michigan was a daughter of Parkholme Crib in whelp to Chineham Young Jack. This bitch had been secured from the English breeder Mr. H. St. John Cooper.

L. E. Furtwangler and John P. Kilgore were joint owners of the Kinderhood Kennels, Greensburg, Pennsylvania. Among their stud dogs was King Pluto, an important winner in England sired by Khumhardi Babi (who was by Ch. Prince Albert). King Pluto's dam was Corsham Bogie (by Graveney Robert, a son of Stockwell). Another heavy-weight stud at this kennel was Ingoldsby (by Hazelmere Prince ex Dame Portland). The third dog was County Chairman, a dog of Stone breeding.

In 1902, Chibiados, a white and brindle dog shown by Mr. E. K. Austin, was first in a novice class of twenty-three entries, with Fashion second. Chibiados then won over Rodney Grabber in both limit and open light-weight Bulldogs, and was reserve to Portland in winners, thus defeating Mersham Jock, a heavy-weight he had not met in his classes. Subsequently, Mr. Austin sold Chibiados, and the following year this winning dog defeated Rodney Stone and Ivel Doctor, who was reserve in winners. At the following show, held at Orange, New Jersey, Rodney Stone was defeated by Ivel Doctor but did win over Chibiados in the light-weight class.

The 1904 New York show as judged by Mr. W. J. Pegg, owner of the Woodcote Kennels in England. Under Mr. Pegg, Chibiados won in his class, defeating every dog he had been placed over in 1903 with the exception of Ivel Doctor, who was first in winners, with a new dog, Sir Lancelot, as reserve. Among the high-class dogs that

Ch. NeMac's Sir James Fearnought,
owned by Nellie S. McFarland.

Ch. Bredt's Top Shelf, owned by Elmer S. Bredt
and Warren B. Adelman.

Chibiados competed against on that occasion were Rolyat and Rodney Smasher. The latter had acquired his championship at an early age and at the same show won the Waldorf-Astoria Cup for the best American-bred dog.

Another winner at the 1904 show was La Roche, then six years old, who won the special for the best bitch in the show, a prize that is not offered today. La Roche, in the 1904 show, placed over her kennel mate, Thackeray Soda, who was also considered a bitch of excellent conformation.

During the same period, Mr. J. Gould entered the fancy and imported a very fine dog at a very high figure. In this case the dog was Heath Baronet, purchased from a Mr. Mills, of Uxbridge, England, for the sum of five thousand dollars.

Beginning their kennels at their home in Wheeling, West Virginia, Mr. and Mrs. Albert Loest, show superintendents, owned and raised Bulldogs for many years. Perhaps their best-known Bulldog was Ch. Moston Gladiator, an English dog that had been imported by John Collins. Incidentally, in recounting the exploits of this dog, Albert told me that at that time only ten points were required to make a champion, and the points awarded at a show were based upon the number of combined entries of all breeds at the show: one hundred entries, one point; two hundred entries, two points; etc.

Another Bulldog imported by Mr. Collins was the excellent Moston Colonel. Other good ones brought to America were Ch. Rolyat, Ch. Berners, Ch. Kentish Lady, Ch. Rodney King, Ch. Shoetown Pride, and Rodney Empress.

Among the outstanding available stud dogs, some of which had been imported, were the good brindle Mersham Ham; Jack Stone, from the famous Stone strain; Ch. St. Vincent and Lord Chancellor, two typical brindles with good English records; Moston Colonel, a Prince Albert-bred dog that had proved himself as a show winner as well as a good sire; Ch. Shoetown Pride; Ch. Thornbury Diamond; Ch. Mahomet and his massive brother Odin; Pitland, a sound heavyweight; Nuthurst Surprise; Young Mahomet; Nairod's Heywood Cerberus; Ch. Rodney King; and Woodcote Hermit.

Among outstanding brood bitches which had proved themselves through their outstanding progeny as well as their winning on the show bench were Ch. Leone Hazelwyn (purchased from Mr. Cooper Mott); Ch. Miss Aubrey; Ch. Vinemount June; Ch. Kentish Lily;

162

Ch. Heywood Beauty; Firenze Belsize; Dundee Pandora; Madam Menelik; Moston Molly; Dame Portland; Princess Nestor; Peggy Stone; Rodney Maple Leaf; and Broxholme Darkie.

The prize-winning American-bred dogs included Mr. Croker's Broadway, Black Maria, Belanshee, and Buccaneer, outstanding Bulldogs descended from Rodney Stone and Persimmon-bred stock.

The people prominent in the Bulldog Club of America from 1902 to 1910, as far as officers and Boards of Governors are concerned, included H. C. Beadleston; R. S. McCreery; W. N. LeCato; Richard Croker, Jr.; W. C. Codman; J. H. Matthews; E. K. Austin; and John Collins. At this time the Club's main activities included the holding of one general meeting of members, and a dinner each year; generous donations of medals to the clubs in the East for the Bulldog classes; the sponsoring of the entry at the Westminster Kennel Club show.

The constitution and by-laws were amended in 1904 and the Club was incorporated. The Club was then recognized by the American Kennel Club as the parent club for all Bulldog specialty clubs. The

Ch. Estrid Jupiter, imported and owned by John O'Melveny, was a noted winner during the late 1960s. *Bennett*

163

parent club gave or denied permission to join the BCA or the AKC; to hold specialty shows; determine championship points and were the custodian of the Bulldog Standard. All of these rights are still controlled by the BCA except the determination of championship points; now determined by the AKC. Also in 1904, dogs that were altered or maimed were declared ineligible for show competition; and in 1914, the Dudley nose was proclaimed as a disqualification.

National interest in the breed grew far beyond the fondest expectations of the fathering group who originated the Bulldog Club of America. The BCA was a loosely-knit organization, recognized by the AKC as the parent club and the governing body of all things pertaining to all Bulldog exhibiting and breeding.

Starting in 1907, and continuing for several years, the Club ran two specialty shows a year, one in New York and one in Philadelphia. Contrary to the present system, the Board in the early years was decidedly opposed to recognition of other Bulldog specialty clubs; only after several refusals and much debating was the Bulldog Club of Philadelphia recognized in 1907, and it was many years before the Bulldog Club of America recognized other specialty clubs.

During this period, McClure Halley's Bredbury Belle did considerable winning, and Leeds Merry Girl, Leeds Saucy Girl, and several others with the Leeds prefix of Mr. Delmont's kennel were also among the winners. The Vinemount dogs, Amber, Dark, and Folly, owned by Mr. Austin, were others that were being shown, as were Ch. Patience and Battle Axe owned by W. R. Goodwin. The Rodney Kennels were winning with such dogs as Ch. Rodney Merlin, Rodney Smasher, Rodney Toreador, and Rodney King. Mr. Haggenjos was showing Dalston Dick, and Master Grif and Donna Donax from the Illini Kennels were other winners. Among the new fanciers were Mr. P. Scardon with Beaming Belle and Rickey; Mr. Hawkins with Bertie's Best; the Rockcliffe Kennels with Crissie Denton; Mr. Saltzgaber with Crumpsall Chief; Dr. John Lehner, with Crumpsall Stym; Billy Drew with Buttons II, Drewstone Pike, and Gaby Deslys; C. P. Boyd with Hewlett King Orry; Harry Ruston with Princess Merlin, Woodcraft Mahomet, and Woodcraft Bertie; and the Dreamwold Kennels and Dreamwold Blunderbus, Dreamwold Juanita, Dreamwold Supreme, Dreamwold Centurion, and Mauvorneen Mica.

164

In 1911, the prominent winners of the Club's specials and trophies for American-bred Bulldogs were Mr. Croker's Bracelet and Broadway, and Mr. Ginsdale's Gotham Belle Victoria; other winners were Mr. Beet's Ch. Mahomets Son; Mr. Roarback's Mlle-Modiste; Mr. Baushliker's Pitlands Son; Mr. Wood's Colony Castoria; Mr. Lederer's Inwall Prodigal and Deerpark Princess; Mr. Coon's Linda Stone; Mr. Murray's Polly Rajah; Mr. Boger's Young Broadway; and Mr. Beal's Penway Paralyn.

1911 was also the year that the English fancier Colonel J. A. Edelston bred the bitch Norton Violet to one of the winning dogs of the day, Chineham Joker. Of the two very good puppies in this litter, Ch. Woodend Joan (a bitch originally known as Norton Tiberia) was discussed in the Chapter on British shows, fanciers, and dogs. The other outstanding puppy was a brindle-pied male which Colonel Edelston named Norton Sambur. Because his owner did not consider him a good tempered dog, Sambur was shown only rarely. When he was two years old, Sambur was sold to Sam Crabtree, who later sold the dog to an American fancier, Alex Stewart. Sambur was shown with great success in the United States and became an American champion under the name of Strathtay Prince Albert. His top win was Best in Show at Westminster in 1913 under the English judge Captain W. R. Beamish. Ch. Centaur was second, Ch. Beaming Blunderbuss was third, and Ch. Deodora Monarch was fourth. Ch. Strathtay Prince Albert was a sound dog of exceptional conformation, particularly for those days, and was the progenitor of some very fine stock. Other imported Bulldogs owned by Mr. Stewart were Strathtay Knowle Marquis, Strathtay Knowle Monarch, and Strathtay Thornwood Kitty, all of whom became champions.

Rockcliffe Kennels' Ch. Oak Nana was imported from the Sturgeon Kennls in England and soon earned her title as an American champion. From the Woollons Kennels in England Mr. J. Davies imported Roseville Brittania, who later went to Dr. Lehner's Crumpsall Kennels. Ch. At Last, a very sound specimen, was imported by Mr. Saltzgaber.

Mrs. C. W. Platt had Astoria Baron; F. K. Pierson, Bill Cerberus; Mrs. W. Hildebrand, Deodora Billy; J. E. Horrax owned Cintra John and Ch. Toll Bar Jack; at the Auburncrest Kennels of Dr. Glen Adams were Warfleigh Nabob, Lord Salisbury, Glenarden Dusky Maid, Ch. Thornton Quiry, and Ch. Auburncrest Challengers Double; Dr. Earl Russell owned Russell White-light, Kamel Park Lillian, Kamel Park Dalien, and Crusader (a son of Irish Alaunt); Ch. Muiravonside Challenger and Ch. Rose Marie (half-brother and and sister) as well as Buccaneer were at the kennels of R. H. McElroy.

Ch. Buccaneer (whelped in 1919 and winner of the 1924 Chicago show) was an imported dog with another impressive pedigree. Among his progenitors were Ch. Prince Albert, Boomerang, Heywood White Marquis, and Wroxham Silent Prince. Mr. McElroy also owned Tytherington Oddy and Tytherington Lancastrian as well as the remarkable Ch. Muiravonside Challenger, whose show record has been equalled by few dogs, and who gained his championship without a single defeat.

Ch. Challenger Cracker, Melbourne Kilmahew, and Mr. Sparkplug were in the Melbourne Kennels of Guy Hornish; Ch. John Citizen, a fawn son of Eng. Ch. Wenden Citizen, and Ch. Colleen Brawn were at the Monte Kennels of Montgomery Purviance; Brantford Fair Play was shown by the Mildred Kennels; Mr. John Haggerty imported Hefty Legacy, who later went to Mr. and Mrs. Earle Smith, owners of Ch. Allah Challenger and later of the imported Hefty's Best. Mr. and Mrs. Fred Ray had British George, Hefty Peggy, Hefty Commodore, Smithdown Evangeline, and Langton Red Marquis.

Ch. Silent White Redcap (by Int. Ch. Glorious Soubriquet ex Silent White Pauline) was among the very good Bulldogs of the time. Bred by William A. Richards and later owned by Mr. A. F. Kramer, Redcap was a red brindle with many of the outstanding characteristics of her famous sire. She was Best of Breed on several occasions, as well as best of all breeds in the Danville, Illinois, and Waterloo, Iowa, shows in the 1920's. Other outstanding Bulldogs from the Silent White Kennels of Mr. and Mrs. Richards were Silent White Duke, Silent White Romance, and Silent White Commodore.

Prince of Ricelands, owned by the Riceland Kennels, Platte Center, Nebraska, was another Bulldog of merit of about the same period. G. H. Hammon (Sparrow Bush Kennels) had Sparrow Bush Sir Don and Sparrow Bush Captain Kidd. Can. Ch. Sandy McNab (by Ch. Kingsway Man O'War ex Viceroy's Cambra Duchess, and owned and bred by T. Cruickshank, Vancouver, B. C.) was one of

Ch. Hooray For Me, owned by Donald and Barbara Thackeray.

McCreery's Tam O'Shanter Morgan, owned by
Richard and Virginia McCreery.

the outstanding Bulldogs of the Pacific Coast. R. W. Baushliker's Hefty Son of Mike was another good specimen of the breed. Ch. Warleigh Nabob was a white-pied owned by B. G. Saltzgaber at the Warleigh Kennels; early in his career, Nabob was purchased by the Auburncrest Kennels.

Ch. Caulfield Billy, sired by the famous Caulfield Monarch, was a winner in England before he was imported by Thomas J. Parvin, Newark, New Jersey. Billy had much of the quality of his sire, who was known as England's best heavy weight of his day. Mr. and Mrs. Parvin later brought out Markham Spot and Temporary Husband, two fine specimens.

Int. Ch. Tufnell Launtett, owed by Kurtis O. Froedtert, completed her championship in England, and after coming to the United States was awarded Best of Breed at Westminster. Roseville Barrie, another fine specimen, was owned by Mr. A. T. Howard, of St. Louis, Missouri. Arbaugh's Micky, owned by A. W. Arbaugh, Portland, Indiana, had an impressive pedigree including a double cross of both Coaster's Diamond and Ch. Heywood Marquis. Ch. Failsworth White Knight and Kilbourne Fascinator were others listed among his progenitors.

Ch. Auburncrest Challenger's Double (a son of the famous Irish Challenger) was another notable specimen of the period. Auburncrest Lord Salisbury, a son of Ch. Challenger's Double, was owned by Glenn Adams, Cincinnati, Ohio, Int. Ch. Challenger Cracker, owned by Dr. L. F. Bacon, Cedar Falls, Iowa, acquired championship titles in both Canada and the United States and proved himself a really great sire.

Ch. Kamel Hefty Legacy was considered one of the outstanding Bulldogs of 1925. Owned by James T. Stephens, this Bulldog made his championship in record time. Int. Ch. Arthur Pen, owned by Walter E. Simmonds, won best in Non-Sporting dogs at three successive shows in the 1920's. Ch. My Dear, a litter sister of Ch. Yamamoto Challenger, was another winner of the times. Muiravonside Dick O' The Main, an import whose pedigree included Irish Alaunt, Ch. Challenger, Pleasant Bertie, and Duranside dogs, proved an excellent sire. Charles S. Webber's Glenarden Sir Resolute was a fine Canadian specimen whelped in 1924. Int. Ch. Dauntless Dan, Int. Ch. St. Roch's Girl Guide, and Ch. Dunalaunt were also among the good Bulldogs in Canada. The latter was sired by Irish Alaunt, as was E. W. Hammond's Regalaunt

Ch. Royal Bone Bandit, owned by Mr. and Mrs. Herbert W. Grueber.

Mr. and Mrs. Thomas Grisdale owned Ch. Sensible Fred as well as Prince of Wales, who was purchased from Charles Webber. An undefeated American and Canadian champion, the latter was taken to England where he was known as Dominion Fortitude. There he won three challenge certificates in rapid succession. Unfortunately, this really exceptional Bulldog met with an untimely death.

The Baumgartners' Baumbrae Kennels in Michigan had Magnet Princess Pat, Baumbrae's Pride of the Hills, and Ch. Hefty's Best. Two imports, Morovian Martini and Woodley Imp (the latter a daughter of Hefty Monarch) represented the basic breeding stock of J. M. Ayers' kennels in Indianapolis. Ch. Silent White Romance (Dr. and Mrs. Wade, Baltimore) and Ch. Captain Doleful (Mr. and Mrs. Wilbur Thornton, Cleveland) were enjoying successful show careers, as were Midwick Challenger (Lostonia Kennels) and Broxton Bandmaster (Broxton Kennels). Alaunt's Cintrason (Mr. and Mrs. Earl Smith) was imported about this time.

Carey Lindsay's Ch. Maple Spring Boddie Boy was whelped in 1926. This exceptional Bulldog (by Regalaunt ex Maple Spring Lady Zetta, and representing the English blood of Irish Alaunt and Kilburn Regal, and the Canadian blood of Ch. Coster's Diamond and Hefty Monarch) was Best of Breed at Madison Square Garden in 1929 and 1930. In 1931 he won the Group and was runner-up for Best in Show. The sire of at least nine champions, Boddie Boy's name is prominent in many pedigrees. Among his get were Ch. Spring Lake Son O' Boddie Boy, Ch. Roxton Buddy Boy, and Ch. The Crovanspring. The latter, owned by Mr. and Mrs. McCroden, was an exceptional Bulldog of the 1930's and was considered one of the best ever bred in America.

Gotham Sensible Fred headed Mr. and Mrs. P. Maude's kennel in Brooklyn. The imported Manresa Molly, one of the greatest bitches ever whelped, was brought out by Reginald Sparkes, who also owned the lovely bitch Westdorf's Miss Cintrason. Ch. Dick o' the Main, shown by Mr. and Mrs. Stuart, had an exceptional show career. And Colonel and Mrs. Robert Guggenheim were represented by Son O' Cinders.

Roxton Irish Boy (Mr. and Mrs. Harry Brunt) and Morovian Marvel (Mr. and Mrs. Ashton) were also prominent at that time. Three fine stud dogs of the period were Morovian Master, Morovian Midshipman, and Morovian Mariner, owned by C. J. Dunlap, Delaware, Ohio. Two other fine Morovian specimens of the early 1930's were Morovian Mainstay (Melbourne Kennels) and Morovian Mounty (owned by Mr. and Mrs. Stuart). Consistent winners were Queen of Challenger (also owned by the Stuarts), Boltonia Barrister (Mr. and Mrs. Lewis), Lorne's Latest (Mr. McGovern), Bonhomie Captain (Mr. and Mrs. Fred Ray), and Morningside Minotaur (Morningside Kennels). Midwick White Knight, Duway's White Marquis, and Sir Major Spike were also in the limelight. Regalaunt (Mr. and Mrs. Brunt) and Regalaunt Heiress (B. L. Booth) were also making names for themselves.

The Canadian Bulldog Dewhurst Dan, owned by Percy Alderstone, was a Westminster winner, as was Queen of Challenger. Morovian Meddlesome (Mrs. Howard B. Hoel) and Sensible Fred of Hamtondale (shown by George Hargreaves) were among other outstanding Bulldogs.

Ch. Jolly Jericho (Ch. Phillips Jolly Atlas ex Ixie's Jewel of Buttonwood) was whelped in 1935. Owned by Mr. and Mrs. D. Fred Phillips, Jolly Jericho had an enviable show record and sired eight champions: Ch. Jolly Janet, Ch. Jolly Jordone, Ch. Tierney's Esquire, Ch. Sunnyledge Showman, Ch. Dusty Vulcan, Ch. Rogers Gentleman Jack, Ch. Sociable Topper, and Can. Ch. Jolly Joker. At the 1946 Bulldog Club of New England specialty show, forty-one descendants of Jolly Jericho were entered, and all were brought into the ring during intermission to honor this exceptional sire.

Two other outstanding Bulldogs of the mid-thirties were the litter brothers Ch. Kempston Beau Ideal and Ch. Kempston Crusader (sire of nine champions) who were bred by Walter Brown, Toronto, Canada. These two dogs were by Int. Ch. Kamel Morovian Mainstead ex Lady Molly.

White Mule was being shown by K. M. Bruce, and later, Mr. Bruce brought out Drinkmoor Moonshine, sired by White Mule. Drinkmoor Moonshine was a great Bulldog who had a sensational show career for a number of years. Ch. Roseville Barrie (Mr. A. T. Howard) was brought out about this same time. Mr. Chetwin showed his Canadian bitch Tiddlie Pom of Coldstream, and somewhat later, Ch. Coldstream Gladiator, another good Bulldog.

A West Coast Bulldog of exceptional merit was Eng. and Am. Ch. Cloverley Bachelor, owned by Stanley Webster. Cloverley Birthday was imported soon after and was shown by Fred King

171

in both the United States and Canada. Two other imports of about the same period were Junior's June and Parkholme Primula, who were exhibited by Mr. Sparkes.

Other winning dogs whose names should be mentioned were Ch. White Marquis and Duway's Dutchess (owned by J. J. Douett); Morovian Mandalay and Morovian Maurice (P. E. Belting); Ch. Charminster Son o' Sandy (a son of Lorne's Latest): Maecliffe Galleon Master and Seven Gables Galleon Master (owned by Mr. and Mrs. De Renne); British Overdraft, owned by Mr. Ballantyne; Seer's Jock's Jockette, owned by Thomas Hayden; Ch. Limehouse Happy Hooligan, owned by Harry Isaacs; Morningside Melvin, from the Morningside Kennels; Ch. Cragsman Buckshot (owned first by Mr. J. Pate and later by Mrs. Millard White, who also owned Ch. Yorkist Leonora); Ch. Mayer's Girl, Vindex Victory, and Falstone Duchess, owned by J. W. Tillet; Basford Ideal, Bunjie, Morovian Mainstead, Kamel White Knight, and Clarinda (Mr. Sparkes); Broxton Bootlegger, Broxton Beloved, and Broxton Brigadier (Broxton Kennels); Vardona Lord George and the litter sisters Vardona Sunny Girl and Ch. Sonny Girl (sired by Ch. Anglezarkes Sonny Boy, and owned by Dr. Vardon); Fernstone Dolly and Fernstone Doris (owned by George Hargreaves); Ch. Basford Elite (Edward M. Wright); Ch. Monica White Knight (Frank Hogan); Sunny Sue of Barnards Green, a Canadian-bred; Eng. and Am. Ch. Vindex Valeria, imported by John Prescott; Ch. Londontown Carthorse (Ben Matthews); Ch. Cambridge Gladiator (Francis J. Thudian); Ch. Ginger Hekantakit, who completed his championship at Morris and Essex under the ownership of William Murray; Ch. Charminster Jolly Bargeman (Richard Trimpi); and five champions of the Sociable Kennels: Sociable Shingle, Sociable Sugar, Sociable Browne, Crew So Fantine, and Crew So Sociable.

Ch. Leatherneck Semper Fidelis (Best of Breed at Westminster) and Ch. Leatherneck E As It were representative of the fine stock of Leatherneck Kennels, Dour Daquiri (a son of Homebrew and grandson of Drinkmoor Moonshine) was being shown by Mrs. Henriquez. Morningside Marmaduke, a Morris and Essex winner, and Morningside Monty were also being shown extensively.

Mrs. Robert S. Horne's Hobbyhorne Cinnamon (Ch. Kamel King of Bundick ex Porch's Country Sweetheart) was whelped in 1939.

This exceptional bitch produced a number of outstanding offspring. Mated to Ch. Dour Dimboola twice, Cinnamon the first time whelped a litter including Ch. Hobbyhorne Georgette and Ch. Hobbyhorne Decorum; the second litter included Ch. Hobbyhorne Hallmark and Ch. Hobbyhorne Home Maid; mated to Ch. Roseville Blazingstar, Cinnamon produced Ch. Hobbyhorne Cinnastar II; mated to Ch. Elvinar's Falstone Torpedo, Cinnamon produced Ch. Hobbyhorne Cintorson, Ch. Hobbyhorne Hedy, and Ch. Hobbyhorne Hussy.

Duranside Roddy, Dour Dockleaf, Dour Dimboola, Dour Disdain, and Morningside Mecca were among the Bulldogs sharing the show honors with such others as Ch. Renown, Ch. Fernstone Dorma, Cragsman Buckshot's Golden Boy and Ch. Basford Playboy.

During the same period, Morovian's Stormer's Draftsman was coming to the fore. This exceptional brindle-pied, bred by F. M. Carmack, was by Roseville Bingboy ex Ch. Morovian Stormerette, and was whelped in 1941. Showing exceptional quality even at an early age, Ch. Morovian's Stormer's Draftsman is perhaps the breed's greatest sire, for he sired at least twenty-three champions. Among his champion get are: Kapra's Saint Hubert, Stormer's Double Draftsman, Ideal of Maple Lodge, Patsy of Maple Lodge, Stormer's Draftette, Draftsman's Miss Stormer, Morovian Stormer's Valiant Lady, Joelen Son-o-Trix, Joelen, Ben Di Mister Bull, Draftsman's Duz, Cogdell's Deborah, Sairey Gamp of Min-T, Charleen's Susie of Draftsman, Can. Ch. Wetchin Brindle Beauty, Picapenny's Glory B, Joelen Delight o' Trix, and Joelen Scion o' Trix.

Falstone Dreadnaught, Morningside Mosaic, Basford British Mascot, Cochisa, Boatswain, Sociable Ronnie, and Duranside Roddy were among the Bulldogs of note. Then in 1946 Albert Farrel's bitch Ch. Nugget Valet's Lady (bred to the imported Rhydian Roger) whelped a litter including Ch. Nugget Trelor, Ch. Nugget Treloress, and Int. Ch. Nugget My Ideal. Trelor became an outstanding sire and produced at least nine champions. Nugget My Ideal was acquired by Joe D. Laughlin and soon became an American and Canadian champion. My Ideal was also a prepotent sire and produced at least eleven champions. He was Best of Breed at the Buckeye Specialty Shows in 1948 and 1949 and at the Bulldog Club of America Show in 1949. He was also Best of Breed at the Bulldog Club of Indiana Specialty and at the Hoosier all-breed show in

173

1950. Among the champions he sired are the following: O'Sandy's Jiggs II, Nuggetaire's Carmetta, Millviews Soda Spike, Rio Rita's Golden Nugget, Double Nugget, Nuggetaire's Huckleberry, Huckleberry Lindy's Nugget, Nuggetaire's Caroline, O' Sandy's Butcher Boy, Huckleberry Lindy's Joy, and Sheridan's Huckleberry.

Late in the 1940's a committee was appointed to investigate and make recommendations on the re-organization of the Bulldog Club of America with a view of making it truly a national organization, representing all sections of the United States.

The committee was made up of the following: D. M. Livingston of Pennsylvania, chairman; Harry A. Brattin of Indiana; Ernest S. Chang of Hawaii; Marie Collins of California; Howard Field, Jr. of California; Carolyn R. Horne of New Jersey; J. R. Lockett of Ohio; Paul Maddux of Indiana; Frederick I. Pratt of Connecticut; Fred Ufhel of Maryland; and Frank D. Carolin of New Jersey as member ex-Officio.

This well-qualified committee presented a new Constitution and By-Laws as we find them today. On February 13, 1950 a new organization was voted into existence by a two-thirds vote of the membership of the Bulldog Club of America. The Club under the new plan was divided into seven divisions, the eighth was later added by a split of one of the divisions, each governed by a Board of Governors consisting of the divisional officers (president, vice-president, secretary and treasurer) and at least three, and not more than five, other members.

The entire club is in turn governed by a council and officers elected by the membership. Divisional officers are elected at biennial meetings of members held in the month of October in each odd-numbered calendar year. The executive committee (officers and councilors) is elected by mail ballot on the third Friday of October in each odd-numbered year.

All officers, councilors and board members serve for a period of two years. The officers of the executive committee (president, vice-president, secretary, treasurer) are chosen from a different division every election. This system has worked very well and great strides have been achieved in the interest of Bulldogs and bulldoggers.

Prior to the reorganization, the Board of Governors conceived the idea that since the Club was a National organization, so should the Club's annual specialty show be a National event. It was believed

Ch. Wixey.

Ch. Kapra's Huberta.

Ch. Harvey's Defender.

175

that this National aspect could be achieved by holding the shows in various sections of the country, thus making them available to all members as well as Bulldog people generally. Plans were developed to make this possible, and on October 1, 1949, the show was held in Indianapolis, Indiana, with the Bulldog Club of Indiana functioning as host for the occasion.

Judge William Tuten of Ellicott City, Maryland, selected Int. Ch. Nugget My Ideal, owned by Joe D. Laughlin, as best of breed, and Ch. Duchess of Milsande, owned by Mrs. Elizabeth W. Ford, as best of opposite sex.

In 1950 the Club's show was held at Santa Monica, California, on September 17th. On this occasion the Pacific Coast Bulldog Club was the host. Robert S. Horne judged the show and selected Ch. Placerita Gold Dust, owned by Mr. and Mrs. R. C. Philbert of Newhall, California, as the winner of Best of Breed honors. The Best of Opposite Sex award went to the Maxmal Kennels' entry, Ch. Wixey, owned by Dr. and Mrs. Malcom E. Phelps, El Reno, Oklahoma.

In 1951 the Specialty show returned to the East, with the Washington Bulldog Club as sponsor. Held at Fort Hunt, Virginia, on April 21, 1951, the show was judged by Mr. Harry H. Brunt, who selected Fred Ufhel's seven-year-old fawn, Ch. Sassy Dan, as Best of Breed and Mr. Leo Dobrzyn's Winners Bitch, Dobson's Water Queen, as Best of Opposite Sex.

The show was moved to the Southwest in 1952, and was held in Dallas, Texas, on November 2nd, with the Lone Star Bulldog Club as host. Dr. John H. Elvin, the well-known bulldogger, judged; he selected Mr. and Mrs. William C. Schrader's Ch. O'Sandy's Jiggs II as Best of Breed and Mr. and Mrs. H. K. Cogdell's Ch. Cogdell's Deborah as Best of Opposite Sex. His selections were made from one of the greatest arrays of champions to be found—a total of twenty-two in addition to Best of Winners.

The Long Island Bulldog Club was host for the 1953 B.C.A. Specialty show, which was held in conjunction with the Westbury Kennel Association's All-Breed Show at Westbury, Long Island, on September 27, 1953. The judge was Mr. William C. Schrader of Sandusky, Ohio. Seventy-one Bulldogs, including fifteen champions, were entered for a total of ninety entries. Winners Dog was Cogdell's Zephyr (owned by Mr. and Mrs. H. K. Cogdell), who was also Best of Winners and Best of Breed. Winners Bitch was Damon Guthery's Rio Rita's Judy, who was also Best of Opposite Sex.

The Bulldog Club of Indiana was the host club for the 1954 show which was held on March 28th in conjunction with the Hoosier Kennel Club all-breed show at Indianapolis, Indiana. The judge was C. L. Savage of California, and there were fifty-two dogs in competition. Winners Dog and Best of Winners was Sandow, owned by Mr. and Mrs. A. R. Glass of Chicago. Winners Bitch and Best of Opposite Sex was Kapra's Huberta, owned by Kapra Kennels (Mr. and Mrs. Buschemeyer) of Louisville, Kentucky. Best of Breed was Ch. O'Sandy Jiggs II, owned by Mr. and Mrs. Schrader of Sandusky, Ohio.

On April 3, 1955, the Bulldog Club of America held its annual Specialty show in New Orleans, Lousiana. Host for the show was The Bulldog Club of Louisiana. There were fifty-eight dogs in the sixty-two entries. Judges for the show were Mr. Roy N. Wingo and Mr. Frank D. Carolin. An interesting side-light of the show was that the assignment for each judge was not known until the day of the show, when the assignments were drawn. Special arrangements had been made with The American Kennel Club so that this could be done.

Mr. Wingo judged the dogs and Mr. Carolin the bitches and all

Ch. O'Sandy's Jiggs II (Ch. Nugget My Ideal ex O'Sandy's Pabette), owned and bred by Mr. and Mrs. William C. Schrader.

inter-sex competition. The Best of Breed honors went to Mr. and Mrs. J. L. Wilburn's Ch. Huckleberry Lindy's Nugget, and Best of Opposite Sex was awarded Mr. Everett S. McNeese's Ch. Hardin's Dagmar. There were five champions shown. Best of Winners for five points was Mr. and Mrs. Brian O'Brian's Boru's Nuggetoro (a son of Ch. Double Nugget out of Rita's Olivia, bred by Mr. Damon Guthery). Winners Bitch for five points was English Classic Charlotte, just a year old in March. Owned by Mr. and Mrs. Gilbert Peart, she was a daughter of English Classic Fagin out of Hanson's Bebe, bred by Mary L. Hanson.

The Bulldog Club of America held its 62nd annual Specialty show at Kansas City, Missouri, February 18, 1956 and was sponsored by the Heart of America Bulldog Club. It was a five-pointer in both sexes. Reggie Sparks of Canada did the judging honors and gave a worthy accounting of himself.

Best of Breed honors went to Ch. Huckleberry Lindy's Nugget, owned by John L. Wilburn (Texas). Best of Opposite Sex, Best of Winners and Winners Bitch all went to Twin Shot Limey, a lovely little bitch owned by Vardona Kennels. Winners Dog went to Smackover Pale Dry Pete, owned and bred by W. H. Irvin (Texas).

The Bulldog Club of Philadelphia acted as host for the 63rd annual Specialty of the B.C.A. on October 6, 1957. It was held in Devon, Pennsylvania, on the Estate of Mr. and Mrs. John A. Yohn, Green Valley Farms, within a few miles of historic Valley Forge.

There was an entry of eighty-seven for Judge C. L. Savage, president of the B.C.A. to pass judgment on. The quality was excellent.

Ch. Mapo's Sandman was selected as Best of Breed and Ch. Bayside Anisette for Best of Opposite Sex honors. Char-Anne's Top Octane was Winners Dog while Pilgrims T. V. Sylvania was chosen as Winners Bitch and Best of Winners.

The Lone Star Bulldog Club of Dallas, Texas, was host to the B.C.A. for its 64th annual Specialty, held November 2, 1958. Ernest S. Chang, noted bulldogger from Honolulu, Hawaii, did the judging assignment and passed on an entry of eighty-five good Bulldogs.

As Best of Breed, judge Chang selected Vardona Kennels' Ch. Vardona Frosty Snowman. Best of Opposite Sex was Mr. and Mrs. Carl L. Fisher's (Nebraska) Ch. Maid of Corn Cob. Winners Dog was Jerohn's Stu-Nought, owned by Mr. and Mrs. John S. Klopfenstein and Winners Bitch and Best of Winners was Pic-A-Zorro June Bug, owned by E. S. Windfield (Texas).

Ch. Fickling's Jeb Stuart, owned by Allison W. Fickling. *Graham*

Eng. & Am. Ch. Denbrough Delos, owned by Dr. and Mrs. Saul Schor and Dennis Shaw.

Ch. Piccadilly's Sand Dollar, owned by Cody and June Sickle.

Ch. Westfield's Alabastrine Stone, owned by Virginia M. and Mrs. Charles A. Westfield, Jr. and shown with Mr. Westfield. *Shafer*

At its best, the dog sport is a wonderful, family activity. Exemplifying this commendable aspect of the hobby are the children of Charles and Virginia Westfield. These youngsters are shown with three of the family's champion bitches. They are (from left): Virginia (now an AKC approved judge), Barbara and Charles. *Shafer*

October 4, 1959 saw the Detroit Bulldog Club hosting the 65th B.C.A. National show in conjunction with the Progressive Dog Club of Wayne County, Michigan. The Club was very fortunate in obtaining as judge, Mr. James Allen of England. Mr. Allen drew an entry of 122 dogs.

Winners were: Best of Breed, Ch. Vardona Frosty Snowman owned by Vardona Kennels. Best of Opposite Sex, Best of Winners and Winners Bitch was Colmey's Kathy Ann owned by Victor Colmey. Winners Dog was Ballindine Brigadier Butch owned by Delia and Bob Livingston, and Reserve Winners Dog Livingston's Lucky Contender owned by Mr. and Mrs. Bob Livingston, and Reserve Winners Bitch Vardona Pocket Piece owned by Vardona Kennels. This was the second year in a row for Ch. Vardona Frosty Snowman as Best of Breed at the National B.C.A. show.

The 66th National B.C.A. show was held in Houston, Texas, on October 16, 1960. Mr. Paul Maddux officiated as judge in the Houston Exposition Building with the Bulldog Club of Texas acting as host. Best of Breed went for the third year in a row to Ch. Vardona Frosty Snowman owned by Dr. Edward M. Vardon, Detroit, Michigan. Best of Opposite Sex and Best of Winners was Lazy B's First Princess owned by Bob and Betty Browne. Winners Dog, owned by Gauthier and Hoagland, was Jerohn Morovian Bronze Boy.

The National B.C.A. show went to the far northwest and was held at Portland, Oregon, on September 30, 1961 in the West Mall Arcade, hosted by the Oregon State Bulldog Club. This was the 67th annual specialty, judged by George Beckett, and drawing a good entry of seventy-eight Bulldogs, twenty-three of them champions. Best of Breed went to the greatest winner in the history of the breed, Ch. Vardona Frosty Snowman, owned and shown by Dr. Edward Vardon. This was Frosty's fourth successive B.C.A. win at the National show. Best of Opposite Sex went to Int. Ch. Gatewood Miss Bar, owned by Joan M. Railton, of North Surrey, B.C., Canada. The Winners Bitch and Best of Winners was Tauntem Fearsome Yemima, owned by Joan Railton. Trumbells Big Muscles, owned by Mr. and Mrs. G. Nettleton, was Winners Dog and this win finished his championship.

This show was a centennial for Bulldogs as it marked one hundred years of showing Bulldogs at dog shows.

The B.C.A.'s 68th National show was held on March 25, 1962 at

181

Indianapolis, Indiana, with 105 entries and C. L. Savage judged with the Bulldog Club of Indiana hosting the show. Winners Dog and Best of Winners was Deborah and Phil Stonehouse's Snowman's Kenilworth Tyke. Winners Bitch was Mapo Kennels' Sandees, Best of Breed was Ch. Vardona Frosty Snowman and Best of Opposite Sex, Bob and Betty Browne's Ch. Lazy B's First Princess. This was the fifth year in succession for Frosty at the National show, a record never equaled and not likely to be topped for a long time.

On Sunday, April 21, 1963, the B.C.A.'s 69th National show with John O'Melveny as judge, was staged at St. Louis, Missouri, and was hosted by the Bulldog Club of Greater St. Louis. There was an entry of ninety-one dogs. The quality was again very good. Best of Breed selected was Ch. Jerohns Stu-Nought and Best of Opposite Sex was Ch. Rawburn Bayside Bayberry; Best of Winners and Winners Dog, Jerohn's I'm Mr. Kelley, with Milkman's Janda of Jerohn going Winners Bitch.

The 70th National B.C.A. show was hosted by the Bulldog Club of Denver, Colorado and was held on April 18, 1964 at the Colorado National Armory. C. D. Richardson judged an entry of 124 Bulldogs. Judged Best of Breed was Ch. Shadow's Smasher owned by Mrs. A. R. Glass and Best of Opposite Sex and Best of Winners, Skookum's Sister Susy, owned by Carmarthen Kennels. Winners Dog was Turner's Replica O' Dreadnought owned by Ervin L. Turner.

The 1965 B.C.A. 71st Annual Specialty show was held on October 16th in conjunction with the Catonsville Kennel Club Show at West Friendship, Maryland. The Capitol Bulldog Club of Washington, D.C. was host club and the judge was William Schrader of Sandusky, Ohio. There was an entry of 106 dogs. Winners Dog and Best of Winners was Glamor Boy Festus O'Pal Dor owned by Mr. and Mrs. Palmer J. Phillips. Winners Bitch was Mrs. Teresa McKeown's Plezol's Gillian who finished her championship with this win. Best Bulldog selected was Vardona Kennels (Dr. E. M. Vardon) Ch. Vardona Snowman's Double and Ashford Kennels' (Mr. and Mrs. J. F. McManus, Jr.) Ch. Ashford Sandstone went to Best of Opposite Sex. Reserve to Winners Bitch was Nugget Lady Capri, a puppy bitch six to nine months, owned by Willits H. Sawyer, and the Reserve Dog, Mrs. A. R. Glass' Sequel Smasherjo, a Bred by Exhibitor cntry.

Ch. Hugh's Pistl-Pete of Kelly Road, owned by Pat and Perry Ropp.

Ch. Brookhollow Gingerbush and Virginia Westfield made a formidable team in Junior Showmanship competition in the early 1970s. They are shown winning in the JS classes at Worcester County under H. J. Weiner. In addition to being half of a great JS team, Gingerbush was a top producer as well being the dam of Ch. Westfield's Flying Colors and the granddam of Ch. Westfield's Cunomorus Stone. *Shafer*

The 72nd annual National B.C.A. show was held at Arcadia, California on April 23, 1966 in beautiful Arcadia Park with the elegant B.C.A. banner swaying gently in the breeze. The host club for this great annual event was the Pacific Bulldog Club of the Los Angeles area.

Mr. Ernest Chang of Hawaii opened the festivities with the Puppy Sweepstakes. Best in Sweepstakes was awarded to Bayside Son of Jade, owned by Dr. and Mrs. Alfred Freedman. Next Dr. Malcom Phelps judged the B.C.A. National Specialty with an entry of 129 Bulldogs from all over the nation. After hours of exciting judging he awarded Best of Breed to Ch. Hetherbull's Arrogance owned by Jeanette and Robert Hetherington, Franklin Lakes, New Jersey; Best of Opposite Sex to Ch. Overfen Helen owned by John O'Melveny; Winners Dog and Best of Winners to Gaylord Sepreme owned by Dennis L. Vener; Winners Bitch to Delaut Bit of Gold Champane owned by Delaut Kennels (Audrey Thomas); and Best Puppy to Gould's Buckie of Kelley Road owned by Beryl Gould. It was indeed a very successful show.

On September 29, 1967 the Bulldog Club of America held its 73rd annual Specialty show in the main ballroom of the Holiday Inn at Plainview, New York (Long Island). Judge James L. Vaughters did the honors with an entry of 106 Bulldogs from coast to coast. Judge Vaughters' selections were Best of Breed Ch. Vardona Frosty's Masterpiece, owned by Dr. Edward M. Vardon, Best of Opposite Sex Ch. Shackleford's Sugar Plum, owned by Delmar Shackleford; Winners Bitch and Best of Winners Ashford Superb Brigid, owned by Ashford Kennels (Mr. and Mrs. James F. McManus Jr.); Winners Dog Averill's Kid Ferdinand, owner Mrs. S. P. Averill. Sweepstakes Judge was Alexander Rae Sr. Best junior and Best in Sweepstakes was Schor's Red Rogue of Boomer, owned by Mr. and Mrs. Saul D. Schor. The best senior was Hetherbull's Arrogant Jr. owned by Mr. and Mrs. George W. Stinger.

Shortly after this great win, Int. Ch. Vardona Frosty's Masterpiece was exported to England, a switch on importing and exporting of Bulldogs. This dog was owned jointly in England by Mrs. J. Mitchell and Dr. Vardon.

Division VIII of the Bulldog Club of America hosted the 74th Annual B.C.A. National Specialty at Memphis, Tennessee on November 29, 1968. Ernest S. Chang of Hawaii was the judge of the

184

Ch. Palamar Hathaway, owned by Mr. and Mrs. Paul A. Langford, Jr.

Ch. Bev-Ron's Mission Belle, owned by John and Sandy Barrow.

145 dog entry which included 36 champions. He selected as Best of Breed Ch. Bayside Doubloon owned by Dr. and Mrs. Alfred M. Freedman; Best of Opposite Sex, Best of Winners, Winners Bitch McGerr's Hopefull Kate owned by Jean and Robert Hetherington; Winners Dog Citizen Stu Jones Mr. Britches owned by Pauline M. Pine; Reserve Winners Dog, B.P. Smasher Joe's Sugarlite owned by Mrs. A. R. Glass and James F. McManus; and Reserve Winners Bitch, Lady Henrietta owned by Harry and Erin Dunn.

The Diamond Jubilee, 75th Annual Bulldog Club of America Specialty was hosted by the Detroit Bulldog Club in Detroit, Michigan on October 6, 1969. There were 133 Bulldogs including 31 champions entered from which judge Miss Iris De La Torre Bueno made her selections.

Mr. Howard Sanford judged the Puppy Sweepstakes class of 14. His top selections were Gordon's Chief White Cloud, owned by Gordon and Sally Schiletz; and Chic-A-Ree's La-Z Da-Z as best female pup, owned by Luree and Eugene Cooper.

Judge De La Torre Bueno's preference was Best of Breed Ch. Min-A-Sota Fats of Kelley Road owned by Beryl and Edith Gould; Best of Opposite Sex, Ch. Taurustrail Blazing Vixen owner Taurustrail Kennels, Reg. (Abe and Suzi Segal); Best of Winners, Winners Dog, Taurustrail Houseboat, owner Frank Pupek; Reserve Winners Dog, Bonafide Lord Snowdon, owner Harry and Blanche Deutsch; Winners Bitch, Gaylord's Golden Amber, owned by Lawrence and Maribeth Potter; and Reserve Winners Bitch Luthein's Sugar and Spice, owner Mary F. Gyles.

Mrs. Gould's Ch. Min-A-Sota Fats of Kelley Road went on to win Best in Show in the Progressive Dog Club's show with an entry of 1231 dogs of 96 different breeds. Not bad for one day's work?

San Francisco was the city and the Bulldog Club of Northern California the host for the 76th annual National B.C.A. Specialty. The date was September 12, 1970. Kenneth R. Branion did all of the judging except the bitch Classes which were judged by Miss Joan M. Railton and the Sweepstakes judged by Albert W. Hentschel. There was a very good entry of 148 bulldogs from far and near.

The judges' selections were as follows: Best of Breed Ch. Min-A-Sota Fats of Kelley Road, (a repeat of his 1969 win) owned by Mr. and Mrs. Beryl Gould; Best of Opposite Sex Ch. Newcomb's Automatic Sender owned by Mr. and Mrs. Robert L. Newcomb; Best of

Ch. Bayside Doubloon, owned by Dr. and Mrs. Alfred M. Freedman.

Ch. Min-A-Sota Fats of Kelley Road, owned by Beryl and Edith Gould.

Winners, Winners Dog Delightful Buck of Kelley Road owned by Mr. and Mrs. Robert Karnes; Winners Bitch Galbraith's Kansas City Kate. owned by Mr. and Mrs. Dave Galbraith; Reserve Winners Dog Brookhollow Frost Bit, owned by Henry L. Franklin; Reserve Winners Bitch Flomar's Arrogant Pawnee, owned by M. E. Hess and Lorana P. Buckland; and the Veterans class winner was Ch. Troth's Crown Jewel Surprise, owner Mr. and Mrs. Paul E. Troth; Sweepstakes winner was Sourmug's Jon Jon, owned by Mr. and Mrs. John Jackson.

The Fort Worth Bulldog Club elected to host the 77th Annual National B.C.A. Specialty on November 5th 1971. The show place was the Inn of Six Flags, Golden Palace, Arlington, Texas. Judge Howard M. Grimm of Washington D.C. was elected to do the breed and Judge Callan S. Riggs of Chatsworth, California the Puppy Sweepstakes.

There was a beautiful entry of 195 with a total of 148 dogs which included 35 champions in the Best of Breed competition.

The Sweepstakes was judged first and the Junior Puppy Bitch, Juggernaut Christmas Melody owned by Rita Little and Mae Nelson was the winner.

Judge Grimm selected for his Best of Breed and Stud Dog winner Ch. Har Jo's Cornhusker Pete, bred and owned by Mr. and Mrs. Harlon Luttrell. His Best of Opposite Sex selection was Ch. Scarlet O'Hara of Blackwatch, (she also has two legs toward her C.D. obedience title), bred by Gwendolyn L. Whitmoyer and owned by Beverly Qualls and Gwendolyn L. Whitmoyer.

Other winners were Winners Dog and Best of Winners Bayside Bonanza owned by Mr. and Mrs. Alfred Freedman; Reserve Winners Dog Hetherbull Arrogant Zenith owned by Mr. and Mrs. Daniel Hetherington; Winners Bitch Schor Red Rogue's Pete-Too-Nia owned by Mr. and Mrs. Saul Schor; Reserve Winners Bitch, Westfall's Outdoors Rebel, owners Mr. and Mrs. Willard Cordrey; Veteran Ch. Schor Schoene Maedel, owners Mr. and Mrs. Saul Schor; Brood Bitch, Ch. Britain's Defiant Heritage, owners Mr. and Mrs. Joe Thomason; and Best Puppy, Brookhollow Journeyman owned by Brookhollow Kennels (Mr. and Mrs. Ernest F. Hubbard).

The Sheraton-Boston Hotel in Boston, Massachusetts was the site of the 78th Bulldog Club of America National Specialty. It was held on December 15th 1972 with an entry of 95 Bulldogs representing

Ch. Har Jo's Cornhusker Pete, a winner of the National Specialty.

Ch. Sourmug's Jon Jon, owned by John Jackson and Robert L. Newcomb, was BB at the BCA Specialty in 1972.

exhibitors from 23 states. There were 29 dogs and 43 bitches entered in regular classes and 23 champions in Best of Breed competition.

Judge Marie Andree selected Ch. Sourmug's Jon Jon as Best of Breed. He was co-owned by Robert L. Newcomb and John C. Jackson. Best of Opposite Sex was Ch. Brookhollow Midnite Express owned by Eleanor M. Hendlowitch.

Winners Dog and Best of Winners was awarded to Amos O'Britan owned by Sam Sciarrabone and J. Patrick Hartle. Winners Bitch was Saxe Gothe Lady Blanche owned by Miss J. Cave.

Reserve Winners Dog went to Capeway Buz of Brookhollow owned by Sharon Pupek. Reserve Winners Bitch and Best Puppy went to Mrs. David W. Barret's homebred Da-San's Molly By Golly.

From an entry of 34 Judge Hamilton Webert selected as Puppy Sweepstakes winner, Bredt's Prima Dona. Best Senior Puppy was Dey-Del.

The 79th annual Bulldog Club of America Specialty was held on September 21, 1973 at the Holiday Inn of Denver-South. There was a record entry of 180 Bulldogs with exhibitors from 26 states. Entries included 70 dogs, 64 bitches, four veterans and 42 Champions entered for Best of Breed competition.

Dean Anderson of Rowland Heights, California judged dogs and intersex competition. Douglas Wilson, of Little Rock, Arkansas, judged bitches.

Judge Anderson selected Ch. Min-A-Sota Fats of Kelley Road for Best of Breed. This was the third National Specialty Best of Breed win for Beryl and Edith Gould's homebred topper. Best of Opposite Sex went to Ch. Summit's Sassy Pants, owned by Ivan and Eva Bean.

Winners Dog and Best of Winners was awarded to Oliver Twist IV owned by Bud Havens. Winners Bitch was Mr. B's Tiny Bubbles, owned by Mary Van Scoyk.

Reserve Winners Dog was Barbara Maines' Sarazan's Gambling Man. Reserve Winners Bitch was awarded to Bull-Land's Bundle of Joy, a homebred owned by Richard and Laura Lee Noland.

Best Puppy went to Dale and Penny Hancock's Hancock's Rock Salt Oscar. Mr. and Mrs. Donald Price's Ch. Smasherjoe's Shadow Buster topped the Veterans Class for Dogs and Bitches. Winner of the Stud Dog Class was Margaret Brownell's Ch. Alken Duncan

190

Ch. Summit's Sassy Pants, owned by Ivan and Eva Bean.

Ch. Jonathan of Riverbrae, owned by Catherine Freeman.

Rowser. Ch. Hetherbull Arrogant Dynamo, owned by Jean and Robert Hetherington Jr. was awarded Best Brood Bitch.

Frances T. Richardson of Cameron, Missouri judged the Puppy Sweepstakes. From an entry of 48 she selected Jc's Jon-Boy Collins owned by James and Corinne Winick as Best Junior Dog and Best in Sweepstakes. Winner of the Junior Bitch class was Harlon and Joyce Luttrell's Rich Bonalu. Best Senior Bitch was Newcomb's Automic Dealer owned by Brenda and Bob Newcomb with Paul and Marian Langford's Palamar Humdinger topping the Senior Dog class.

The 80th annual Bulldog Club of America Specialty was held at the Royal Coach Motor Inn of Atlanta, Georgia on October 18, 1974. A record entry of 199 Bulldogs from 29 states and Puerto Rico were on hand for the event. Entries included 82 dogs, 69 bitches, three veterans and 43 Champions entered for Best of Breed competition.

Ernest Chang of Honolulu, Hawaii judged dogs and intersex competition. Colonel Bailey C. Hanes of Santa Fe, New Mexico judged bitches.

Judge Chang's selection of Winners Dog and Best of Winners, Serenade's Mack the Knight, went through to Best of Breed. This two-year-old dog was bred by Daniel Coffey and owned by Bruce Riendeau. Best of Opposite Sex went to Ch. Bettebus Calamity Jane owned and bred by Buster Wilson.

Winners Bitch was awarded to Fog E. Bayes owned by James and Myra Bayes. Reserve Winners Dog was Guy and Iva Mosley's Bronco Linebacker Two. Reserve Winners Bitch was E. J. Little Red Nellie Girl, owned by Edna and Clifford Stebbins.

Best Puppy went to Aubry Foster's Chianti Sipper of Westbriar. Harry and Blanche Deutsch's Ch. Bonafide Double Delight topped the Veterans Class for dogs and bitches. Winner of the Stud Dog Class was Ch. Golden Carmel Coach, owned by Mr. and Mrs. Larry A. Nelson. Ch. Hetherbull Arrogant Dynamo, owned by Jean and Robert Hetherington was awarded Best Brood Bitch.

Mrs. A. R. Glass of Northbrook, Illinois judged the Sweepstakes. From an entry of 70 Bulldogs she selected Shack-A-Jewell Maude, owned by W.C. Jewell and Delmar Shackleford as winner of the Senior Sweepstakes class and Best in Sweepstakes. Topping the Junior Sweepstakes class was Aubry Foster's Chianti Sipper of Westbriar.

Serenad's Mack The Knight, owned by Mr. and Mrs. Bruce Riendeau, was BB from the classes at the BCA 1974 Specialty. *Graham*

Ch. Kyleken Chunk O'Nugget, owned by Kyleken Kennels.

Ch. Nobb Hills Molly Pitcher, owned by Kathy Smith.

Ch. Marinebull's All The Way (Ch. Golden Carmel Coach ex Ch. Marinebull's Here She Comes) owned by Karl and Joyce Dingman and bred by Frank A Cox, Jr. This dog cut a huge swath in the wins column in the late 1970s. Owner-handled, he was fearlessly campaigned in many parts of the USA against all comers. He accounted for numerous Specialty, Group and BIS victories and was the finalist from the Non-Sporting Group at the 1978 Westminister show — only the fifth of his breed to top the Group at this distinguished event since 1930.
50 Catch

The Bulldog Club of America's 81st annual National Specialty was held in Seattle, Washington on September 26, 1976. There was an entry of 111 Bulldogs. All the regular classes were offered, with classes for Best Puppy Stud Dog, and Brood Bitch.

Mrs. Nora Morton of Worcester, England judged and selected as Best of Breed Ch. Marinebull's All the Way owned by Karl and Joyce Dingman. Best of Opposite Sex went to Ch. Dynamo's Rebecca of Wicklow owned by Patricia Kennedy. Best of Winners and Winners Bitch was Vintage Simone owned by Jill Kniess and Dennis Arayou. Winners Dog was Kralan's Moby Dick owned by Dub and Adele Irvin, and Reserve Winners Dog was awarded to Bull-Land's Tuff Stuff owned by James and Sharon Baldwin, Draper, Utah.

Eugene Hahnlen, Woodinville, Washington, judged the Sweepstakes. From an entry of 23 he selected as Best Puppy NeMac's Sir James Fearnought, owned by Nellie McFarland, from the 9 – 12 months Puppy Dog class.

The Stud Dog class winner was Ch. McCreery's Tam O'Shay, owner Richard and Virginia McCreery and the Brood Bitch class winner was Duncan's Eleanor of Aquatine owned by Callan Riggs.

During America's Bicentennial Year, the Bulldog Club of America held its 82nd National Specialty show in King of Prussia, Pennsylvania on October 3rd 1976. Twenty-five states were represented by the 233 Bulldogs entered with all regular classes offered and also classes for Veteran Dog, Stud Dog, Veteran Bitch and Brood Bitch as well as Sweepstakes.

Judge Richard R. Maze of Houston, Texas selected as Best in Sweepstakes Smasher's Constant Comment, owned and bred by Karl Foester and Ray Knudson.

Judge Charles H. Bain selected Ch. Marinebull's All the Way, owned by Karl and Joyce Dingman, for Best of Breed. Best of Opposite Sex was Ch. Sugarlite's Baby Doll, owned by Karl Foester and Ray Knudson, Winners Dog and Best of Winners was Sir Reginauld of Downing, owned by James Peros. Reserve Winners Dog and Best Puppy was the Sweepstakes winner, Smasher's Constant Comment. Best Veteran Dog was Ch. Shelbyhaus Ragan's Bully Also, owned by Mrs. P. O'Neil Ragan and Best Stud Dog was Am. and Can. Ch. Golden Carmel Coach, owned by Mr. and Mrs. Larry A. Nelson.

Judge Wallace J. Newbill's selection for Winners Bitch was Mary Margaret of Kelley Road, owned by Happy Ann Bridges. Reserve Winners Bitch was Da-Sans Molly's Sugar Bear, owned by David and Sandra Barrett. Best Veteran Bitch was Britain's Queen O'Hearts, owned by Howard and Louise Burt and Best Brood Bitch was Ch. Marinebull's Here She Comes, owned by Frank Cox, Jr.

The Bulldog Club of America's 83rd National Specialty show was held on September 9th 1977 at Bloomington, Minnesota, with judge Nan Burke doing the honors in dogs and intersex and Mrs. Gertrude Freedman passing on the bitches.

Mrs. Burke's Best of Breed was Ch. Baltic's Toughe' Nuff, owned by Dr. and Mrs. John Lusins. Best of Opposite Sex was Ch. Juggernaut Martha Jo owned by Dennis Ehntholt and John Little. Winners Dog and Best of Winners was Naughty Rojo Baretta, owned by John West. Winners Bitch went to Rich Gentle Iodine, owned by C.D. Richardson, scoring from the Puppy class.

Judge Dick Markley selected Dingman's Alley Oop, owned by Joyce Dingman, as Best in Sweepstakes.

Reserve Dog was Wellington's King Louis owned by James and Louise Neary and Reserve Bitch was His and Hers Maggie of Delta, owned by Dick and Nancy Paul. Best Veteran Dog was Ch. Golden Carmel Coach, owned by and bred by Mr. and Mrs. Larry A. Nelson, while Best Veteran Bitch was Ch. Ragan's Hillary Highstep, owned by Jean S. Witt. Ch. Marinebull's All the Way, owned by Karl and Joyce Dingman won the Stud Dog class, and Ch. Lady Laura, owned by Mr. and Mrs. Everett Earley was Best Brood Bitch.

The 84th annual Bulldog Club of America National Specialty show was held on October 8th, 1978 in Southfield, Michigan. The judges were Mr. Delmore Sikorske for dogs and intersex competition and Mr. Stephen Averill for bitches. There was a combined entry of 195 which included 76 Dogs, 98 Bitches, and 51 for Best of Breed (30 dogs, 21 bitches).

For Best of Breed Ch. Bronco's Linebacker Two, owned by Mr. G. H. Mosely, was Mr. Sikorske's selection. Best of Opposite Sex was Ch. Lebo's Peaches owned by Cody T. Sickle. Winners Dog went to Ragan's Toobridge High Haas owned by Carolyn Ragan while Winners Bitch and Best of Winners was awarded to Ms. Prissi Krissi owned by Jerry and Kathy Pritchard. The Veteran Dog selected was Ch. Amhist Nathan Hale, owned by Neil Ragan. Best

Ch. Baltic's Toughe Nuff, owned by Dr. John O. Lousins.

Ch. Rich Gentle Iodine, owned by C. D. Richardson. *Petrulis*

Veteran Bitch was Iron Mike's Lady Mathilda owned by Blair Brininger. In the Stud Dog class, Ch. Marinebull's All the Way, owned by Karl and Joyce Dingman went all the way! Ch. Lebo's Peaches followed her BOS victory by topping the Brood Bitch class.

Sunday, September 16th, 1979 at the Holiday Inn in Charlotte, North Carolina was the date and place of the 85th annual Specialty show of the Bulldog Club of America. There were 238 Bulldogs entered with a total of 328 entries including 85 Dogs, 99 Bitches and a Best of Breed class of 30 Dogs and 24 Bitches.

Judge James R. McIntyre selected as his Best in Sweepstakes, Billyhops Southern Revenge owned by Frank Hopkins and Mr. and Mrs. J. S. Montgomery. Judge Harry Deutsch selected Billyhops Double Darling, owned by Mr. and Mrs. J. S. Montgomery as Winners Bitch and Darlene Stuedmann's Beauty Boogie Oogie as Reserve Winners. His Veteran Bitch selection was Ch. Westfield's Cunomorous Stone owned by Mr. and Mrs. Charles A. Westfield.

Judge James L. Vaughters, Sr. made the following selections; Winners Dog and Best of Winners, Orean Brosam's Shackleford's Tank Too; Reserve Winenrs, Mr. and Mrs. J. S. Montgomery's Billyhop's Southern Revenge: Veteran Dog, Carolyn Ragan and Walter Bishop's Am. and Can. Ch. Amhist Nathan Hale; Best of Breed, Jean Heterington's Ch. Dingman's Hunk of Hetherbull, Best of Winners, Orean Brosam's Shackleford's Tank Too; Best of Opposite Sex, Mr. and Mrs. Charles A. Westfield's Ch. Westfield Cunomorous Stone and Best Puppy in the classes, Billyhops Southern Revenge, owned by Frank Hopkins and Mr. and Mrs. J. S. Montgomery.

A Bulldog Club of America Hall of Fame was inspired by an oil painting of Champion Cockney Gorblimey displayed at the B.C.A. show in Oregon in 1961. The beautiful painting awakened the

Ch. Dingman's Hunk of Hetherbull, owned by Jean Hetherington, was Best of Breed at the Bulldog Club of America Specialty in 1979. *Painting by Jackie Balog.*

Ch. E. J. Little Red Nellie, owned by Edna J. and Clifford Stebbins.

desire of the bulldoggers present to preserve for posterity the great Bulldogs who were winners of Best of Breed at the annual Bulldog Club of America Specialty shows each year. The picture was again shown at the B.C.A. banquet the next year in Indianapolis. Those present gave unanimous approval of the idea.

Meanwhile the dream was being drafted into reality for a Bulldog Hall of Fame Gallery by the able team of Mr. and Mrs. C. L. Savage and was unveiled to the B.C.A. The plan was approved, and the Bulldog fancy began to gather funds to paint the eight Bulldogs winning the Best of Breed since the reorganization of the B.C.A. in 1948.

The oils were painted from magazine pictures, snapshots and photographs by the fine animal portrait artist, D. K. Dennis. Research for the paintings was made by Herm Taylor.

The gallery is made up of the following Bulldogs: Ch. Nugget My Ideal 1949, owner Joe D. Laughlin; Ch. Placerita Gold Dust 1950, owners Mr. and Mrs. R. C. Philbert; Ch. Sassy Dan 1951, owner Fred Ufhel; Ch. O' Sandy's Jiggs II 1952 and 1954, owners Mr. and Mrs. W. C. Schrader; Ch. Cogdell's Zephyr 1953, owners Mr. and Mrs. K. Cogdell; Ch. Huckleberry Lindy's Nugget 1955-56, owners Mr. and Mrs. J. L. Wilburn; Ch. Mapo's Sandman 1957, owners Mapo Kennels (Richard R. Maze and L. J. Poth); Ch. Vardona Frosty Snowman 1958-1959-1960-1961-1962, owner Vardona Kennels (Dr. Edward M. Vardon); Ch. Jerohn Stu Nought 1963, owners Mr. and Mrs. John Klopfenstien; Ch. Shadow's Smasher 1964, owner Mrs. A. R. Glass; Ch. Vardona Snowman's Double 1965, owner Vardona Kennels (Dr. Edward M. Vardon); Ch. Hetherbull's Arrogance 1966, owners Mr. and Mrs. R. Hetherington, Jr.; Ch. Vardona Frosty's Masterpiece 1967, owner Dr. Edward M. Vardon; Ch. Bayside Doubloon 1968, owners Dr. and Mrs. Alfred M. Freedman; Ch. Min-A-Sota Fats of Kelley Road 1969 – 1970 – 1973, owners Mr. and Mrs. Beryl Gould; Ch. Har Jo's Cornhusker Pete 1971, owners Mr. and Mrs. Harlon Luttrell; Ch. Sourmug's Jon Jon 1972, co-owners Robert L. Newcomb and John C. Jackson; Serenade's Mack the Knight, 1974, owner Bruce Riendeau; Ch. Marinebull's All the Way 1975 – 1976, owners Karl and Joyce Dingman; Ch. Baltic's Toughe' Nuff 1977, owners Dr. and Mrs. John Lusins; Ch. Bronco's Linebacker Two 1978, owned by G. H. Mosley; and Ch. Dingman's Hunk of Heatherbull 1979, owned by Jean Hetherington.

Ch. Cockney Gorblimey (Ch. Basford Revival's Replica ex Cockney Duchess).

Ch. Mapo's Sandman, owned by Mapo Kennels.

Ch. Sandow's Smasher, owned by Mrs. A. R. Glass.

English and American Ch. Blackshot's Captain Cook (Ch. Outdoor's Kippand ex Denval Ruffles), owned by Dickensbrae Kennels and bred by Mrs. V. E. Wigley. He is shown winning Best of Breed at the Bulldog Club of Texas Specialty under the author. This dog, handled by Rex Vandeventer, has won more Best in Show awards in all-breed competition than any other Bulldog in history.

Joint Affair, an English import, owned by Dickensbrae Kennels.

This gallery is on exhibition at each of the National Specialty shows for enjoyment and study of the fancy.

The Bulldog Club of America publishes a report every two years which is distributed free to all members. In book form this report contains all of the activities, shows and data of each individual club, with other information of interest to members.

A representative number of kennels, dogs and owners follow: Mr. and Mrs. Raymond L. Dickens (Dickensbrae Kennels), Bulldog owners and breeders for over fifty years, have owned some really great ones, including their English-bred Ch. Morovian He's A Mainstay (George). Among their other English imports were Morovian Newlo Bill, Ch. Falstone Katafelto, Ch. Red Roger of Wiggin (Roger), Ch. Noway's Bodie, Ch. Bowcrest Paddy of Brewick and Ch. Red Boomerang of Wiggin. Mr. and Mrs. Dickens have imported a total of 43 Bulldogs from England. Two of their latest to come over are Ch. Turoca Sea Breeze and Joint Affair.

A more recent import was the gorgeous bitch, Eng. and Am. Ch. Jackath Silver Cloud, who proved to be a great winner as well as a good brood bitch. She was the top winning Bulldog female in 1965 and 1966 with an all-breed Best in Show and eleven Non-Sporting Group firsts.

The Dickens' greatest import was the Bulldog champion of champions, Eng. and Am. Ch. Blackshot's Captain Cook (Cookie). Cookie was shown 89 times and was 42 times Best in Show, all breeds, 74 times first in the Non-Sporting Group and 88 times Best of Breed. He was the top-winning Bulldog in 1966 and the second top-winning dog in the Non-Sporting Group. In 1967 he was top-winning Bulldog and second top winning dog in the Non-Sporting Group. In 1967 he was top-winning Bulldog and second top winning dog in the Non-Sporting Group. However 1968 was Cookie's banner year as he was again top-winning Bulldog, second in Non-Sporting Group and #9 among the Top Ten dogs in the nation on the Phillips System.

He was shown from February 26, 1966 until his retirement on September 5, 1968. He holds the world record of winning more Bests in Show than any Bulldog in history.

I had the unique pleasure of judging the fabulous Cookie at the Bulldog Club of Texas 1966 Specialty in Houston. Now I have had the opportunity to judge and study all three of the Bulldog greats, Fearnought, Frosty and Cookie.

Dr. and Mrs. Malcom E. Phelps, owner of Maxmal Kennels have made a great showing with Ch. Poker Alice, Ch. David's Bathsheba, Ch. Morningside Mosaic, Ch. Maxmal Climax and Ch. Wixey. The latter held a unique show record. Shown 67 times, this dog made 65 trips to the winners' circle. His final tally included two all breed Bests in Show.

Ch. Sir Reilly of Kilarney, owned by George E. R. Morris, was an excellent homebred. John O'Melveny of Los Angeles has imported and made up a number of champions. These included Eng. and Am. Ch. Banshee of Beechlyn, Eng. and Am. Ch. Overfen Helen, Eng. and Am. Ch. Qualco Marksman and Eng. and Am. Ch. Thydeal Relentless and Ch. K-Jo's Christmas Sunshine.

Mapo Kennels, owned by Richard P. Maze and L. J. Hines Poth of Houston, Texas, have conducted a very successful show and breeding program over the years. Ch. Santiago de Batangas, Ch. Mapo's Patty, Ch. Mapo's Sandman, Ch. Ellerie's Easter Sonnet of Mapo (import), Ch. Dax, Ch. Mapo's Monica and last but far from least, Ch. Smashers Souvenir have carried the Mapo banner.

Mrs. Nan S. Burke (El-Nan Kennels, Reg.) has owned and bred some good ones; Ch. El-Nan's Impossible Piranha was #10 Bulldog and top winning bitch in 1968. Ch. Denbrough Leo, Ch. El-Nan's Happy Lollipop and her latest CH. Kralan's Charming Charlie, #4 Bulldog in the country for 1978 and #1 for 1979 are representative of her breeding and showing.

E. S. Winfield did a fine job of breeding and showing with Pic-A-Zorro Bulldogs. Mr. and Mrs. William C. Schrader (O'Sandy Bulldog Kennels) had a great one in their Ch. Cockney Gorblimey. Dr. Elvin's Ch. Elvinar's Falstone Torpedo, Dr. Edward M. Vardon's Am. and Can. Ch. Vardona Frosty Snowman, America's top Bulldog for the years 1958 through 1961 and Dickensbrae Kennels' Eng. and Am. Ch. Blackshot's Captain Cook are long gone now but all will be long remembered.

Dr. Edward M. Vardon (Vardona Kennels) will be long remembered for his many contributions to the breed. He owned, bred and showed such specimens as Int. Ch. Draftsman's Choice O'Vardona, Eng. and Am. Ch. Hefty Upstart O'Vardona, Eng. and Am. Ch. Altonian Snowstorm O'Vardona, Ch. Stomer's Double Draftsman, Tri. Int. Ch. Hefty Red Duchess, Am. and Can. Ch.

Ch. Kralan's Charmin' Charlie, owned by Nan S. Burke achieved national prominence as a strong winner in breed, Group and BIS show competition was #3 Bulldog on the *Kennel Review* system in 1978.

Vardona Ideal Snowman, Am. Can. Eng. Ch. Vardona Frosty's Masterpiece and of course the immortal Am. and Can. Ch. Vardona Frosty Snowman. Frosty sired over a dozen champions and was the winner of 38 all-breed Bests in Show, 119 Group Firsts and 40 Specialty Bests of Breed, the breed record. He was Best American-Bred in Show at Westminster in 1959 and Best Non-Sporting there in 1960. Frosty ranked as top Bulldog from 1958 through 1961; Top Non-Sporting Dog, 1958 through 1960; #7 nationally among all breeds in 1958 and 1959; and #6 nationally among all breeds in 1960. He passed away in 1966 and his great master followed him in death on January 31, 1971; the loss of two great troopers.

Mr. and Mrs. A. R. Glass owned some great ones in Ch. Samson's Souvenir, Ch. Sandow's Smasher and their last Ch. Smasher's Souvenir. Mr. and Mrs. Horne's Hobbyhorne Bulldogs included such specimens as Ch. Hobbyhorne Cinterson and a host of others. Mr. and Mrs. R. C. Philbert's Ch. Placerita Gold Dust was a top show winner.

Maric Bulldog Kennels (Mr. and Mrs. H. C. McElhinny) were well represented by Ch. Pabbie's Pride, Ch. Marmac's Bold Venture and Ch. Marmac's Bold Kate. Ch. Kapra's Saint Hubert, owned by John B. Buschemeyer was another good specimen as was Floyd Lanham's Eng. and Am. Ch. Marquis of the Hills and Mr. and Mrs. A. R. Forbush's Ch. Lonarch British Mascot. Sallybett Kennels owned by the Livingstons had many good dogs including Roger Jerily, Getson Linda Son and Grand Pops Boy. George E. Hargreaves of Fernstone Kennels owned and handled top Bulldogs for many years. One of his best was Fernstone Butch.

Another of the "oldtimers," Mr. Fred King, owned Kingsdale Kennels. He owned and exhibited such outstanding dogs as Cloverly Birthday, Drinkmore Whiskey and the great Eng. and Am. Ch. Duranside Roddy, said by many American judges to be the best Bulldog they had seen up to that time. Among other outstanding dogs were George E. Morris' Ch. Sir Reilly of Kilarney, Mr. and Mrs. C. D. Richardson's Ch. Rich Pilgrim Beans, Ch. Rich Smoky Blackface, Eng. and Am. Ch. Kippax Dreadnought, Ch. Rich Buckshot and Ch. Rich Gentle Iodine.

Mr. Randolph T. Bankson's Ch. Falstone Brindle Duchess, Mr. and Mrs. Paul Maddux's Ch. Ideal of Maple Lodge, Ch. Mim-Jim's Buckie Too of Cha-Ru, Ch. Chia-a-Ree's Buckaroo and Ch. Frazier Copper Jiggs, and Mrs. Gilbert Peart's English Classic Kennels,

American and Canadian Ch. Vardona Frosty Snowman (Ch. Vardona Student Prince ex Ch. Twin Shot Limey), owned and bred by the late Dr. E. M. Vardon. An all-white, Snowman was a consistent threat in all-breed competition in every part of the country. He is shown winning Best of Breed at the Buckeye Bulldog Club under the author. Dr. Vardon always handled the dog in competition and this team swept to some of the most coveted dog show honors. In addition to his being a top show dog, Snowman was also a successful sire with 14 champion get to his credit.

American and Canadian Ch. Vardona Snowman's Double, owned by Vardona Kennels.

American and Canadian Ch. Vardona Ideal Snowman, owned by Vardona Kennels.

English and American Ch. Kippax Fearnought (Ch. Koper Kernel ex Kippax Ann), owned by John A. Saylor, M.D. and bred by Harold Dooler, is remembered as one of the all time greats of the breed. An English champion at the time of his arrival in the United States, he won the Non-Sporting group at the Westminster Kennel Club in 1954 from the open class and returned the following year to capture Best in Show there. This win made him the first Bulldog to win Westminster since 1913. Fearnought also excelled as a producer with a record of 31 champion get.

with Ch. Julius Caesar, Ch. Barney Rudge Fagan and Ch. English Classic Hamlet, are still another group of excellent, well-known dogs.

Other breeders who should be included in any list of outstanding Bulldog fanciers and breeders are: Mr. and Mrs. Charles T. Nelson Jr., owners of Ch. Dynamite of Plumbrook and Ch. Hycard's Fearnought Jacque; Mr. and Mrs. A. J. Therault, owners of Mickey Bulldog Kennels and Ch. Mickey's South Paw and Ch. Showman's Maxmillian; Charles and Hellen Griff, owners of Ch. Griff's Tardy Lad, Ch. Griff's Scarlet Baby and Ch. Griff's Gemo; and George J. Imig, owner of Ch. Honest John.

Dr. John A. Saylor (Fearnought Kennels) imported a great one in his Eng. and Am. Ch. Kippax Fearnought. Bred by Harold Dooler of Manchester, England, "Jock" completed his English championship at the early age of one year and six days. This great dog arrived in America in December 1953 and went Best in Show at Los Angeles at fourteen months, just ten days after arriving in California. He completed his American championship at Westminster in 1954 where he won the Non-Sporting Group. At the 1955 Westminster show Fearnought proved his exceptional worth when he was awarded Best in Show by Mr. Albert E. Van Court. He was shown 29 times, won 17 Bests in Show, and 23 Non-Sporting Groups and the Pacific Coast Bulldog Club's Special Stud Dog Class in 1955, 1956, 1957, 1958 and 1959. I judged this class in 1958 and had the pleasure of examining this great dog. Ch. Kippax Fearnought was much used at stud and proved to be a great producer.

Mrs. Gladys Creasey imported the outstanding Eng. and Am. Ch. Juneter's Ace in October, 1953. He was first shown in America six days after his arrival and fourteen days later he completed his American championship. He was Best of Breed at five successive all-breed shows, Best in Show three times, and second in the Group twice.

Our own Ch. Dicken's Golden Nymph (Sooner) finished his championship in four major shows at only twenty months. He finished at the Lone Star Specialty in 1951 for five points under Judge Paul Maddux. Enroute to his championship he was Best Non-Sporting dog at the Oklahoma City Kennel Club show in 1950. Judge Frank Carolin selected him as Best of Breed from an entry of nearly

209

fifty at the Heart of America Specialty show in 1951. We also owned Ch. Hanes' Little May, a homebred bitch who was defeated only twice on which occasions she went Reserve. She also had a number of Bests of Opposite Sex and was Winners Bitch at the 1954 Lone Star Specialty for four points.

More recently Charles and Eileen Westfield have produced two very outstanding Bulldogs in their Ch. Westfield's Flying Colors and Ch. Westfield's Cunomorous Stone, both great winners. Joan Fisher has an outstanding homebred in her Am. and Can. Ch. Show Biz Fairy Prince. Her Show Biz Forom's Hysterium is also a noteworthy specimen. Many excellent Bulldogs and devoted fanciers have become active in recent years. Others continue strongly in the breed. Some of these and their dogs are Dave Williams with Ch. Harjo's Miracle Babe and Ch. Babe's Tina Maria Coqueta; Mr. and Mrs. Donald B. Thackrey's Ch. Hooray For Me; Carolyn and Neil Ragan's Toobridge High Hass; Ancil G. and Nedra M. Morton's Morton's Buddy; Doug Wilson's Ch. Barcarole Elizabeth; Dr. Saul and Edythe Schor's Eng. Ch. Denbrough Delos, Ch. Sundance Pete-Trie, and Ch. Bowcrest Burma Boy; Cody and June Sickle's Ch. Lebo's Peaches, Ch. Cherokee's Angus of Primeva and Ch. Cherokee Klondike; Bob and Jean Hetherington's Ch. Dingman's Hunk of Hetherbull, Ch. Hetherbull Arrogant Lazarus, U. D. and Ch. Hall's Cudoc Boy; Karl and Joyce Dingman's Ch. Tha-Mac's Stormy Gal, Ch. Dingman's Spooky Ol' Alice, Ch. Marinebull's Kaydee Too, C. D. and the outstanding Ch. Marinebull's All the Way, a top owner-handled BIS and Specialty winner; Carl Riggs' Ch. Perro De Presa Paco; Steve and Ameila Averill's Averill Boatswain Lamb Chop and Ch. Averill Bo'Sun Mutton Chop; Karl Forester and Ray Knudson's Ch. Smasher's Constant Comment; Ernest and Pauline Pine's Ch. Pine's Husker Chop; Mrs. Paul Ukena and Mr. Frank Hopkin's Ch. Ukena's Dingo Rinkles; Doris W. Boyd and Ruth Lee's Ch. Oh Beau Day Scious Me and Pritchard and Dingman's Ch. JK's Miss American Pie. A host of others deserving honorable mention are not included because of limited page space. They have all done their share on behalf of the breed.

The outstanding breeders and kennels in Canada, past and present, include Michele and Perry Nesbitt (Queensbury); Sid Lowings' Ch. Astley of Ludgershall; Mrs. Elizabeth G. Lynch's Ch. Merrywinkle Sharose Bee Bee; Mr. and Mrs. R. E. McCutcheon's Can. and Am. Ch. Kamel Electric Trick; Reginald P. Sparkes' (Kamel

Ch. Westfield's Cunomorus Stone, owned by Barbara and Mrs. Charles A. Westfield, Jr. and bred by Virginia M. and Mrs. Charles A. Westfield, Jr. was one of the breed's most outstanding all-time winners. "Puzzle's" records includes 38 BIS, 22 Specialty BB and 140 G1s. She is also a member of the BCA national gallery of winners and was owner-handled throughout her entire, illustrious career. *Klein*

Ch. Pine's Husker Chop, owned by Ernest and Pauline Pine, was a noted winner and one of America's top Bulldogs in the late 1970s. He is shown winning the Group at Colorado Springs KC under Mrs. Robert Ward, Mr. Pine handling. *Cott*

Who says you can't have fun with a show dog? Here Ch. Pine's Husker Chop takes time to clown between victories. *Francis*

Ch. Show Biz Fairy Prince, a multiple BIS winner, bred and owned by Joan L. Fisher. He is shown with his handler Henry Helmar. *Klein*

Ch. Oh Beau Day Scious Me (Ch. Alpine's Mi Amigo Cisco ex Ch. Amber's Delight Flomar) owned by Ruth C. Lee and bred by Doris Boyd, is a multiple Group winner and the top bitch for 1978 and 1979. She is shown in a BB win under judge Robert Hatch, handler Alvin Lee. *Bennett*

Ch. Dey Del, owned by Robert B. Kullman and handled by Henry Helmar, was only the fourth Bulldog in recent history to win the Non-Sporting Group at the Westminister Kennel Club show. "Baron Siegfried" scored this memorable victory in 1974 under judge Graham Head of Australia.

Ch. Bredt's Ace in the Hole, owned by Mr. and Mrs. Elmer Bredt is a homebred with some distinguished wins to his credit including BB at the 1980 Westminister KC show.

Ch. Smasher's Souvenir, owned by Mapo Kennels.

Ch. Shrink A Bull Ms. Ego, a winning daughter of Ch. Show Biz Fairy Prince, owned by Linda Teitelbaum. *Ashbey*

Kennels) Eng. and Can. Ch. Altonian Supermist and Eng. Ch. Broadford Foden Esquire; Mr. and Mrs. Roy Dewbury's Ch. Kent's Little John, Ch. Blockbuster Baby Ben, Ch. Kempston; George Lammiman; Ruth Bowman's Bowman Kennels, Reg.; and Joan M. Railton; Christopher Heilson; Grace Hutchison and Gary Fredrick.

Mexican dog shows continue to be popular on the Pacific Coast. The shows of Club Canofilo de Baja California are held at Ensenada, B.C., Mexico. They make an enjoyable vacation as well as offering a two-show weekend to compete for a Mexican championship.

There are also a number of championship shows held each year in or near Mexico City, D.F. This also makes the finest of vacations for anyone. Mexican championships are not based upon "points" but rather upon modification of the English certificate system. For the past 30 years the F. C. M. (Federation Canófila Mexicana) is the Mexican organization that conducts dog shows in Mexico and also issues points for Mexican championships. The championship requirements are that the dog must be 12 months of age or older and be the winner four times at four different shows.

The F. C. M. is affiliated with the F.C.I. (Federation Cynologique Internationale) of Belgium. The F.C.I. issues international championships. To win an international title a dog must be at least 15 months old and win four times on the international circuits. These shows are held in Mexico twice each year, in the Spring and Winter.

Once each year the F.C.I. organizes a show in different countries to give a world championship. It awards four titles, world champion dog, world champion bitch, world champion young dog and world champion young bitch. In May 1978 the competition was held in Mexico City and in 1979 in Switzerland.

The Club de Bulldog Ingles A.C. was recently organized in Mexico and will be affiliated with the F.C.M. It is hoped this club can vigorously represent the breed in Mexico.

Mexican champions and their owners are as follows: Ch. George Patton, 1973, Alejandra Moran de Ayala; lCh. Dickensbrae Ben's Ellen, 1973, Maria Elena Macias de De la Toree; Ch. Churruca Zugasti, 1974, Carlos Agosta; Ch. Dicken's Big Ben's Ophelia, 1974, Martha Ann McAlister de Rodriquez; Ch. Tata Goodman's, 1974 and Ch. Jimmy Lee's Chip, 1974, Englentina C. de Duenas; Ch. Twinen's Cleopatra, Michael and Nellie M. Nemeth; Hetherbull Arrogant Merlin, 1974, Bruce and Theo Hollenback; Oliver Canito

Mexican Ch. Jimmy Lee's Hope's Sherry, owned by Ikerne Zugasti
De Garmendia. *Montoya*

Sayles Buckwheat Spats, owned by Jorge Sanchez Gallegos is shown going Winners
Dog at the 1978 Working breeds show in Mexico. Mexico is a member of the FCI and so
Bulldogs at Mexican show are classified as guard dogs. *Montoya*

Huntington Hope Chamar Aru, owned by Gonzalo Alcazar.

Mexican and International Ch. Jimmy Lee's
Touch of Class, owned by Foster Hanson.

Mexican Ch. Huntington Hope Bedar
Asha, owned by Gonzalo Alcazar.

Mexican, International and World Ch. Evelyn, owned by Gonzalo Alcazar.

Cromwell, 1974, Marcela Guajardo; Jimmy Lee's Little Le Roy, 1975, Alberto Castellas; Xochitl Baltazar, 1975, Luis Ruben Baltazar Aceves; Ch. Merlina, 1976, Jesus Arellano; Ch. Dusty Ivanhoe, 1976, Adriana Portillo; Ch. Zaza Agosti, 1976, Vicente Rivapalacio Sulser; Ch. Pug Duenas, 1977, Englentina C. de Duenas; Ch. Jimmy Lee's Hope's Sherry, 1978, Ikerne Zugasti de Garmendia; Ch. Snow White Lady, 1977, Maria de Lourdes R. de Alcazar; Ch. Broncas Touch Santillan, 1978, Mario Hernandez Olvera; Ch. Lady Godiva D. Campo Giro, 1978, Guadalupe G. de Saldana; Ch. Syles Buck Wheat Spats, 1978, Jorge Sanchez Gallegos; Ch. Big Morgan Princess, 1978, Manuel Figueroa Solis; Ch. Socrates De La Torre, 1978, Julio R. Dondish; Ch. Liz Polar Princess, 1979, Jorge Sanchez Gallegos; Ch. Liz Ginger Babe, 1979, Lalie Mendez Zaga; Ch. Huntington Hope Bedar Asha, 1979, Gonzalo Alcazar and Ida Cohen; and Billy Tiger Bosco De La Lama, 1979, N. Elizondo and N. de la Lama.

Mexican and international champions and owners are as follows: Ch. Candy Crosswinds, 1973, Sergio and Noemi Mancisidor; Ch. Dickensbrae Big Ben's Batman, 1974; Ch. Jimmy Lee's Touch of Class, 1975, Foster Hanson; Ch. Lady Zugasti, 1975, Guadalupe G de Saldana; Ch. Huntington Hope Chamar Aru, 1979, Gonzalo Alcazar.

There are but two Mexican, International and World Champions. The dogs and owners are: Ch. Jimmy Lee's Palamar Goldmark, 1978, I. Zugasti de Garmendia and I. Ch. Evelyn, 1978, Gonzalo Alcazar, Evelyn was also female world champion and Goliat De La Torre was the young dog world champion. However this young dog is not as yet a Mexican or an International champion.

Mexican, International and World Ch. Jimmy Lee's Palamar Goldmark, owned by Ikerne Zugasti De Garmendia, was BIS at the Zootecnica show in 1979 under the Canadian authority Mrs. J. H. Daniell-Jenkins. *Montoya*

Americans continue to be a prime market for British-bred Bulldogs. About 25% of the English champions exported come to the United States with an occasional one going to other parts of the world. Japan is Great Britain's second best market with Canada, South Africa, Australia and other parts of the world importing an occasional champion. Bulldogs that are not champions are also in demand and go to about the same places as the champions. Most of these dogs are campaigned in the countries where they are imported and become champions in that country.

A large number of Bulldogs, many of them champions from the United States have found a ready market in Japan at very fancy prices. There are now a number of breeders in Japan and the Bulldog is popular at the Japanese shows.

Locally-bred, good Bulldog puppies in Japan bring from $500 to $1000 if sired by an American champion. If sired by a Japanese champion the cost ranges from $300 to $600. Most good Bulldogs in Japan are direct descendants of American champions.

There were three Bulldog Specialty shows held in Japan in 1978. All were held in or near Tokyo. During this same year there were 270 all-breed shows with entries averaging from 300 to 400 dogs. The largest show of the year was sponsored by the Japan Kennel Club and had an entry of 2500 dogs. The membership of the Japan Kennel Club is now over 35,000. Currently the J.K.C. is organizing a Bulldog division to replace the old All Japan Bulldog Club that has been disbanded.

The popularity of the Bulldog has dropped off some in the last few years but bulldoggers still register around 2000 each year with the Japan Kennel Club.

The following Bulldogs have made important contributions to the breed in Japan during the past six or seven years: Am. Ch. Bar M's Huckleberry Fuzz, Am. Ch. Wicklow's Malibu Sundancer, Am. Ch. Jimmy Lee's Touch of Class, Am. Ch. Judana's Lost Dutchman, Am. Ch. Dingman's Drummer Boy, Can. Ch. The Hannslow Beau, Am. Ch. Jay-O-Gads Jason, Am. Ch. Christie's Flaming Gold, Am.

222

Japanese Ch. Kendee's Edward of Excel Buche, one of Japan's best.

Japanese Ch. Super Sun of Columbine House.

Japanese Ch. Aian of Sunny Kinoshita.

Japanese Ch. Fightman of Pacific Royal Momma.

Ch. Royal Bone Bandit, Am. Ch. Dingman's John Henry, Am. Ch. Tuffnuts Tintack, Am. Ch. Dingman's Alley Oop, Am. Ch. San Sue's Candy Bear and Am. Ch. Baltic's Tough E'Nuff. These dogs should probably contribute much more to the breed during the years to come.

Although the question of a change in the Standard has been discussed a number of times by the Bulldog Club of America during the past ten years it seems to be the consensus of opinion that the Standard has stood the test of time and should not be changed. It has been suggested that the Bulldog should be bred to the Standard instead of changing the Standard to fit the dog.

Ch. Señor Hoss, bred by Mr. and Mrs. Marvin L. Turner and owned by Mr. and Mrs. James D. Hammond, has to date made the greatest impact on the breed in Hawaii as a sire.

Bulldogs in Hawaii

THE Bulldog Club of Hawaii was organized in 1939 and held its first Specialty Show in 1945 and for the next ten or twelve years the Club had a show annually.

Finally the club was dissolved due to a scarcity of Bulldogs and a lack of interest. These shows usually drew an entry of about 30 dogs. In 1952 there were more Bulldog Champions of record in Hawaii than there were champions of any other breed of dogs, and each of these Bulldogs made its championship in Hawaii.

Ernest S. Chang is probably the longest-standing Bulldog fancier in the Islands. He is also an A.K.C. judge of the breed and has judged many times on the mainland and in the islands.

In August 1969 a group of bulldoggers held a meeting in Thomas Square for the purpose of forming a club. Ten interested families organized to spearhead the effort and application was immediately made to the A.K.C. for approval of the club. The A.K.C. gave its approval for the new club to hold licensed shows after the completion of the required sanction matches and the Hawaiian Bulldog

227

Ch. Jo Mar's Red Minx Pal Joey, owned by Mr. and Mrs. Marvin L. Turner, is shown winning a Non-Sporting Group first under judge Derek Rayne, Mrs. Turner handling. *Chun*

Ch. Bruno XIX, owned by Alfred and Laverne Freitas, is shown winning BOS at the 1978 Hawaiian Specialty. *Johnson*

Club held its first licensed Specialty show in 1973. Ernest Chang did the judging honors at the inaugural show. Since then the club has held a Specialty show each year, with the exception of 1975. Entries at the Hawaiian Specialty usually average about 15. There are a total of seven all-breed shows on the Islands each year with an entry of from six to 15 Bulldogs. The scarcity of shows in Hawaii and generally small Bulldog entries at the shows make it difficult to make up a champion.

Due to the quarantine imposed on all dogs entering the state of Hawaii from the mainland and all foreign countries, except England and Australia, it is difficult to bring in new stock or take one's dogs to show on the U.S. mainland. Every dog must be quarantined for a period of 120 days upon arrival in the state and kenneled in facilities located in Halawa Valley. The cost to the owner is now $302.00 and this fee is expected to be revised upward again soon. This rule is a real deterrent to bringing in new blood, consequently very few Bulldogs are imported to Hawaii.

A representative number of Bulldogs and breeders follow: Major and Mrs. Carl Keith, Ch. Keinan St. Nicholas, C.D.; Major and Mrs. Marvin L. Turner, Jo-Mar's Red Minx Pal Joey, Señor Hoss; and Samantha the Minx; Mrs. Ray Tompkins, Keinan Eve's Angel; Miss Kit Woodruff, Schor's Red Rogue's Grandson and a new English import, a lovely bitch, Baylor Swingalong from Arthur Westlake's Kennels, and Mr. and Mrs. Bill Dubb's Keinan Lund Jolly Swagman. Miss Shirley Sumic, owner of Valleyvale El Tigre, and Valleyvale Sunglow from the Valleyvale Kennels of Australia. Valleyvale Sunglow is the grand-daughter of Eng. and Am. Ch. Blackshots Captain Cook.

Since 1972 the following Bulldogs have finished their championships in Hawaii: Ch. Jo-Mars Red Minx Pal Joey, 1972, bred and owned by Mr. and Mrs. Marvin L. Turner; Ch. Samantha the Minx and Ch. Señor Hoss, 1973, littermates, owned and bred by Mr. and Mrs. Marvin L. Turner; Ch. Bruno XIX, 1975, owned by Alfred Freitas; Ch. Bridgette's Heather, 1979, bred and owned by Hank and Roselle Whittington.

Two dogs imported during the late 1970's, Clark's Morris of Alohaisle owned by Shirley and Alfred Kando and Ringmaster Big Shot owned by Richard Ebia, Jr. hold good potential for the Bulldog's future Hawaiian development.

Baytor Swingalong, bred by Arthur Westlake and owned by Hazel Woodruff.

Torro's Tiny Tempest, owned and bred by Hazel Woodruff.

Ch. Samantha the Min, owned by Peter Wong.

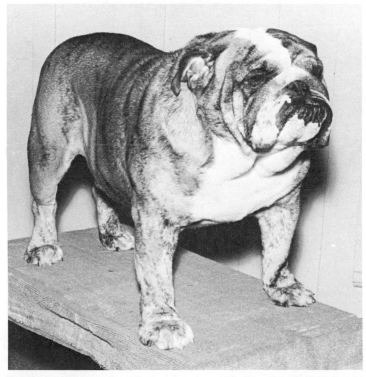

Ch. Keinan St. Nickolas, C. D., owned and bred by Nancy Jane Criss.

The Hawaiian Bulldog Club held its 1979 Specialty show on March 2nd at Thomas Square in downtown Honolulu. The judge was Mr. Terry Collicutt of Tasmania, Australia. Mr. Collicutt judged an entry of 12 and selected Bridgette Heather, owned by Henry and Ronalee Whittington, for Best of Breed and Clark's Morris of Alohaisle, owned by Alfred and Shirley Kando, for Best of Opposite Sex.

Two obedience dogs also finished in Hawaii during the late 1970's: Lord Riki C.D.X., 1976, owned by Melvin and Helen Lum, the first Bulldog in Hawaii to earn the C.D.X. degree, and Gaspro Die Fledermus C.D., 1979, owned by Marion Follmer.

Bloodlines in the islands are very similar to those found on the mainland. This is due to the fact that most of the dogs came from the mainland and England, the same basic source of all our Bulldogs.

In the history of the Bulldog in Hawaii there have been many memorable happenings. One of these was the visit of the Tasmanian judge Terry Coillicutt to officiate at the 1979 Specialty. Here the dogs entered pose in a group photo with their faraway visitor. Mr. Collicutt is shown at the extreme right of the group. *Chun*

Bulldogs in Obedience

IN the last twenty years considerable interest has been shown by a number of bulldoggers in showing Bulldogs in obedience. Most felt that the Bulldog was just as intelligent as the next breed; however, the public seemed to feel the breed was a little on the slow or stubborn side. With this in view a few of the more determined fanciers set out to prove once again that our breed is as smart as the next.

Bulldog owners take genuine pride in their dogs when they enter them in obedience. It gives one the feeling of accomplishment as you and your dog work together as a team. This is also a very fine way to get the breed before the public and improve his image.

It has been estimated on good authority that it takes five shows in the California area to get a C. D. title, twelve shows to get a C.D.X. degree and twenty shows to get a U.D. degree.

Regular classes most offered at obedience trials are Novice A and B, Open A and B, and Utility A and B.

The Bulldog Club of Northern California gave its first obedience trial at its Specialty show on September 11, 1970 in San Francisco, California. The trial had an entry of nine Bulldogs. This is believed to be the first Bulldog obedience trial ever held in the United States.

233

Thunder of Zebulon Pike, U.D., owned by William F. Tisdell, was only the fifth Bulldog to earn a Utility degree.

Ch. Flarepath Splash Gordon, C. D. X., owned by Jim and Susan Werth.

Mrs. Ruth Davis judged this first obedience trial. This club held its second trial on September 18, 1971.

Mr. and Mrs. John Ingley of this club finished their Ch. Ellenberger's Cholmondely, C. D. in January 1965.

Several Bulldogs have successfully finished to the title of Utility Dog, the highest degree in obedience. To name a representative number: Anglo Saxon Gaiety acquired her degree in June 1955, owner Mr. and Mrs. Samuel Gardner; Mar-Jons' Foozie in September 1957, owner Mr. and Mrs. Douglas Dundock, Stormy Day Ginger in June 1970, owner Mr. and Mrs. William McGrath; and James L. Harryman's Chabot's Pugnacious Princess in August 1970.

Members of the Saint Paul–Minneapolis Bulldog Club are also Bill Tisdell's Thunder of Zebulon Pike in October 1971. Now we have the first champion Utility Bulldog in history in Ch. Hetherbull Arrogant Lazarus, owned by Bob and Jean Heatherington. The

Chabot's Pugnacious Princess, U.D., owned by James L. Harryman.

Ch. Ellenberger's Cholmondely, C.D., owned by John and Josephine Ingley.

Nix's Cameo White Fang, C. D. X., owned by Richard A. & Elizabeth E. Fisher.

Stormy Daz Ginger, American U.D., Canadian C.D.X., owned by Mr. and Mrs. William E. McGrath.

Hetheringtons also own Ch. Marinebull's Kaydee Too, C.D. Mr. D. Short also has a U.D. in his Pepper Lady.

Other obedience owners and dogs that should be mentioned are: Mr. and Mrs. Sutter's Sir Charles' Lady Cathryn; Mr. and Mrs. William J. Haralson's, Michael Jay II; Nan S. Burke's Ch. El-Nan's Startling Piranha; John Breece's Breece's Fancy Candie Chief, (a C.D. at the tender age of eleven months and one day in 1972). Other C.D. dogs are Barbara and Jerome Meek's Spunky Grindl Snapper C.D.; Jack A. Westcott's Lady Tabatha Samantha C.D.; Bernard and Janet Secor's Pixie's Lil Golden Nuggette, C.D.; Carol and Edward Leiner, Jr.'s Maximilian Excalibur, C.D.; Richard and Elizabeth Fisher's White Fang Merry Sue, C.D.; Anthony G. Lewis' Lew's Sir Bernard, C.D.; Johnny Young's Valiant Van Buren, C.D.; Marc Trandum's Ch. Cherokee Brahma Sequel, C.D.; Anne M. Palmer's Ch. Bull Path's Ampirion Marigold, C.D.; Mrs. Lawrence Lundburg's Pixie's Marshmallow Butch, C.D.; Becky and Larry Harstad's Larbec's Amber Rose, C.D.X.; Richard and Elizabeth Fisher's White Fang's Snow Bear, C.D.X. and L. Brannan's Ch. Branlynn's Duke of John, C.D.X. In 1976 Lord Riki, owned by Melvin and Marlen Lum of Hawaii, earned his C.D.X. degree. In 1979 Gaspro Die Fledermus, owned by Marion Follmer of Hawaii became a C.D. and Jim and Susan Werth's Ch. Flarepath Splash Gordon earned his C.D.X.

Each year it would seem that more people are taking an active interest in developing Bulldogs in obedience degrees even after the dogs have become conformation champions.

Ch. Turoca Sea Breeze, owned
by Dickensbrae Kennels.

Ch. Gaylord's Heavy Duty, owned by Dennis Verner.

Hints for the Novice Bulldogger's First Show

By Mrs. Carolyn R. Horne

TRAINING a Bulldog for exhibition is not a specialized education. The requirements for a show dog are obedience and good behavior, excellent physical condition and careful grooming—equally desirable attributes for pet or champion.

Before taking a dog into the ring, don't rely on a flurry of preparation just before the show. Handler and dog both need practice and training. The dog must learn to stand quietly and gait easily on leash without tugging or lagging. He should be accustomed to handling by you and by others. Experience in strange environments and acquaintance with other dogs will help him to remain calm and poised in the noisy confusion of a dog show. If you have done your job well, he has thoroughly enjoyed his education and hasn't become bored. You understand each other.

Beautiful condition also comes from faithful care and there is no last-minute substitute. Daily walks keep a Bulldog hard and fit,

239

with stubby toe nails and compact feet. With regular grooming, his coat is shining and healthy; his wrinkles are free from soreness and ugly tear-stains.

When you enter the ring, be as calm as possible. Nervousness transmits itself to your dog and will disturb him. Forget yourself! Think of your dog! Always keep one eye on the judge and be alert to his requests. The judge has only a brief time to examine your dog, make every minute count. Don't stand between your dog and the judge—an invisible dog never won a blue ribbon.

The proper position for a handler is on the dog's right side and, in gaiting, the leash is held in the left hand. But be dexterous from any angle; it's a big advantage.

Always lift your Bulldog with one hand between the hindlegs and one between the forelegs, supporting the bulk of his weight with the hand under the brisket. Don't (please) use his loose skin as a handle and never control his head by clutching the dewlap. Use your hands as little as possible—a light touch is much to be preferred to a tight grip, which encourages the dog to lean or sag. If you can handle your dog well from a standing position with leash control, you have mastered a rare art.

Ch. Hanes' Little May, owned by Col. and Mrs. Bailey C. Hanes.

The Novice Showman

IF you are a novice in Bulldogs and want to show and win there are a few things you should do. My advice would be first: join a local Bulldog club and the B.C.A. Next, carefully look over the field of experienced Bulldog breeders in your locality. See who is well-liked, respected and who shows and wins consistently. Go to him and tell him you are new at the game. An experienced bulldogger will usually help you over the rough spots until you get your feet on the ground.

Study the photographs of the present and past greats of the breed in magazines and breed books. Study the pictorial Standard as well as the written Standard. How does your dog compare with the Standard? What does your breeder friend think? If both answers are "yes" you probably have a better than average specimen.

Now prepare for the show and the acid test. If you have never shown a dog before, look in one of the dog magazines and find out where the next show near you will be. Write the superintendent for entry blanks. Carefully fill them out and return to the superintendent with the required fee and well in advance of the closing date.

Condition and groom your dog for the show. Feed him twice

daily, after exercise, a good dog meal mixed with a pound of fresh ground beef and suet. Give him all he will clean up readily. Each day while it is cool walk your dog. Begin with a block or two and work it up to at least a mile. Take him where there are other dogs, where people congregate in crowds and where there are all sorts of strange sounds, so he will not be shy on dog show day.

Clip his nails, keep them short and brush him daily. Be sure he is vaccinated as your veterinarian recommends. With scissors carefully remove any extra hair in the ears, on the flanks, and around the tail.

At every opportunity pose your dog and make him obey your command to stay. Have everyone you come into contact with handle your dog after you have posed him. Never play with your show prospect and never allow others to.

Take your dog to all the sanction matches or training sessions prior to the first show you can make. Sanction matches are informal practice shows. No points are awarded and entries can be made at the door. The entry fees are low and the whole atmosphere is directed at training novice owners and dogs starting show careers.

Ch. Dickensbrae Silver Spurs (Ch. Clitheroe Kid ex Ch. Jackath Silver Cloud), owned and bred by Dickensbrae Kennels.

Ch. Pic-A-Zorro Abe, owned by E. S. Windfield.

You must decide if you want a professional handler for the first time or so until you become familiar with the routine. If you feel you cannot afford a handler, get a friend with experience to do the job for you. It you wish to show your own dog, there is no better experience for you or your dog and no faster way to learn to handle properly.

Arrive early at the show and be sure your dog is perfectly clean, well-groomed and with all of the whiskers cut off. You may need help with grooming the first time or so. It is always wise to watch others groom their dogs. Never insult the intelligence of a judge with a dirty dog.

When your turn in the ring comes be on hand and ready to go in. If possible get next to an experienced handler, pose and move your dog as he does his entry but be mindful of your dog's individual faults and virtues. Eventually you will master the fine art of handling.

As a parting word of advice do not pay any attention to the pre-show rumors of who will win and who has the show fixed. These rumors are always present and seldom true. Good luck.

Ch. Astley of Ludgershall, owned by Sid Lowing.

Bulldogs in Hot Weather

I HAVE had puppies less than an hour old fret with the heat. Dip a towel in cold water and wring out the excess, spread it out and place the puppies on the damp towel and they will quiet down immediately. Do not place near an open window with a strong breeze or turn a fan on them.

If the mother dog is restless, give her a cold wet towel and a pan of ice. As pups demand it, they can have cold towels until three weeks of age. After that age, you may set a pan filled with ice cubes in their box and they will crawl close to the pan, or away from it, to their own personal temperature control. Watch the eager beaver, for if the pan is shallow, he may crawl into it. The heat seems to bother pups less from three months of age to a year old.

Regardless of how well you think your Bulldog's breathing ability is, there are days with high humidity when he will naturally pant and if allowed to pant for several hours, his throat will naturally become swollen and his air intake restricted. If he gets to the point where he is making peculiar noises in his throat; sides convulsive; tongue off-colored; refuses to drink water or lick ice; he is in trouble and needs your immediate attention. With prolonged panting, he

245

Ch. Jay-O-Gad's Jara Jan, owned by Mrs. J. O. Puckett

Ch. Hefty Red Duchess. Photo courtesy of the late Edward M. Vardon.

becomes congested with a thick ropy white froth or foam. In this, he does not have the ability to vomit thus clearing his throat for the better air intake. To clear his throat, you can reach in and pull this thick mucous out, or use lemon juice, or about half a bottle of 7-up, and this cuts all the phlegm loose, causing the dog to vomit. After this, he should be wet down with cold water and ice packs put on his head; kept quiet until he settles down and is asleep.

Last summer I returned home to find one of my dogs unconscious with a heat stroke. I pried her mouth apart, wedging ice cubes between her teeth to reduce swelling in the throat, as well as to cool her down, also placed an ice pack on top of her head. I kept running cold water over her for almost an hour before she came to and got to her feet. Then she showed signs of shock, so the vet was called. She was given a shot for shock and heat stroke, whereby she quieted down and went to sleep. She awoke four hours later quite normal with the exception of a very sore throat from excessive panting. Once a Bulldog has suffered a heat stroke, they seem much more susceptible to heat.

If you are traveling with your Bulldog, an open wire crate is excellent and will be most useful. You may leave the windows down without danger of suffocation, if you leave the car, nor is there any danger of the dog jumping out. Wet towels, plastic bags of ice cubes or ice bags placed in the crate keep him cool and very comfortable. Any Bulldog that does not like to travel should not be taken for any distance during hot weather. Carrying an ice chest filled with ice, lemon or 7-up may be a lifesaver. Fill quarts or half-gallon waxed milk cartons with water, and freeze them. These do not melt down so quickly as ice cubes.

Never allow children to run and play with a Bulldog during the heat of the day. If temperatures are in the upper 80's, the dog needs to be in a basement with a cement or tile floor, or any place where he will not pant excessively.

A few years ago, we had daytime temperatures from 112-117 degrees. An opening was made under the house, where the dogs crawled down and dug holes in the cool dirt. It was a big relief to hear them snoring.

Again, if there is trouble, first clear the dog's throat manually, or with lemon juice, then use ice cubes in a pack and cold water; if the dog is unconscious, CALL THE VET.

247

Ch. Blondie Beauty, owned by Darlene Stuedemann.

Breeding by Vaginal Smears

by Jerry L. Watson

MOST Bulldog breeders will concede that the conception rate is low among our bitches. I believe that this low conception rate is due in part to the fact that many Bulldog bitches ovulate abnormally, i.e., other than between the 10th and 13th days. By using vaginal smears, one can easily detect optimum breeding time in the bitch. I have bred bitches as early as the fifth day of their seasons and as late as the 20th day using vaginal smears, and conception occurred. I know of incidences where the bitch was bred even later. Bitches that ovulate early will often continue to discharge and remain in heat for several weeks. It has been my experience that these bitches, unless they are older, are not receptive to the male at breeding time. Older bitches will often be receptive for as long as a week before they are ready to breed. Also, I have found from experience that bitches rarely conceive on the same day from one litter to the next. As an example, one of my own bitches was bred on the eighth and ninth days of her cycle for her first litter; the 13th and 14th days for her second litter; and on the fifth day for her third and final litter. From careful observation I am sure of the exact days. A number of my older bitches had been bred every time they came in heat, yet they never conceived until vaginal smears pinpointed optimum time. One such bitch had ten puppies.

Vaginal smears are beneficial even where conception problems do not exist. Vaginal smears indicate when to breed, but just as importantly, they show when not to breed. If one has two or more bitches that come in heat at approximately the same time and only one stud dog is to be used on all, one can easily determine which bitch is more advanced and breed that bitch first. I have bred as many as three bitches to the same stud on three consecutive days, and each bitch conceived. Had they been bred in any other order, conception might not have occurred; however, this is purely an academic question, since conception resulted from each mating. Early examination of the vaginal smear can often detect an infection. If a breeder wishes to ship a bitch, he might change his mind if such an infection were to be discovered. However, some bitches with infections still conceive. I will discuss this later.

In order to do smears, the breeder must have a microscope. A microscope that has at least one low power magnification (100x) and at least one high power magnification (400x) is recommended. A microscope with a variation of these powers might do just as well. The low power magnification is used to examine the overall view of the smear and the high power is ideal for close examination. In addition, one needs microscopic slides, slide covers, long cotton swabs (not ordinary swabs), and new methylene blue stain. (Heartworm diagnostic stain by Pitman-Moore is the same or similar.) These supplies can easily be obtained from your veterinarian.

To make the smear, clean the external genitalia of the bitch. Spread open the vulva and insert the swab past the vestibule well into the vagina (under the base of the tail). Rotate the swab gently before withdrawing it. "Roll" the smear firmly onto a clean slide. (One complete roll is sufficient.) Put a drop of new methylene blue stain on the slide cover and invert the cover onto the smear. Using this method of staining, the smear must be examined immediately as deterioration begins within a few minutes. There are other methods of collecting and staining the smear, but the above method is simple and very satisfactory for the purposes of the breeder.

With the onset of proestrus (the first sign of heat) the estrogen level begins to rise in the bitch and continues through estrus (receptive stage). Vaginal smears measure the estrogen level, and the

Ch. Marinebull's Kaydee Too,
owned by Karl and Joyce Dingman.

Ch. Edwards' Tuffy Gangbuster, owned by
Francis and Barbara Edwards.

Ch. Tha-Mac's Stormy Gal,
owned by Karl and Joyce Dingman.

bitch ovulates at estrogen peak,[1] provided there are ova to ovulate. Ova are not fertilizable immediately following ovulation,[2] and there is a time lag between actual ovulation and vaginal cellular response. The purpose of this discussion is to pin-point *optimum breeding time*, not ovulation per se.

With the increase of estrogen levels in the bitch, the cells from the vaginal smear progress from non-cornified cells (normal, rounded cells) to cornified cells (dead, flat-sided cells).[3] With the disappearance of estrogen, the non-cornified cells return, and the bitch goes out of heat (metestrus). There are four main types of cells, with variations of each type, seen in the vaginal smear. First, there is the parabasal cell—non-cornified with a large nucleus (slide A). Next, there is the intermediate cell—cornified or partially cornified with a smaller nucleus than the parabasal cell (slide B). Next, the superficial cell—cornified with a very small nucleus or a nucleus that appears to be dividing (slide C). Finally, there is an anuclear cell—a cornified cell with no nucleus (slide). These four types of cells appear roughly in the order stated—parabasal, intermediate, superficial, anuclear. Optimum breeding time occurs when practically all the cells in the smear are cornified, anuclear cells. However, there are other conditions necessary for conception to occur. After the height of estrogen effect, i.e., full cornification of cells without nuclei, the cells in the smear return to all parabasal cells within twenty-four hours, or in some bitches the change gradually occurs over several days before the entire smear reverts to parabasal cells. White blood cells may or may not be present at this time.

In slide E, the pointer is on a leukocyte (white blood cell). There are several types of leukocytes, but this type, the neutrophil, is seen most often in the vaginal smear. The other types are very similar in appearance and easily distinguishable. Leukocytes may be present in proestrus and again when the bitch is "out" (out for optimum breeding time, possibly still receptive); but there are no leukocytes present at optimum breeding time. Erythrocytes (red blood cells) may or may not be present throughout the cycle and have little or no effect on reading the smear. Red blood cells are very small compared to white blood cells and usually are not visible using new methylene blue stain. Therefore, don't worry about red blood cells when examining smears.

Slide F shows the smear of a bitch that has been out of heat for

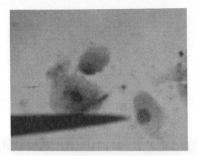

Slide A

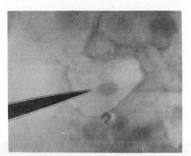

Slide B

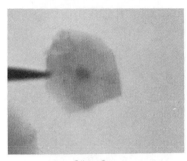

Slide C

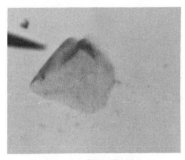

Slide D

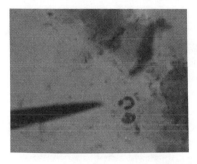

Slide E

Slide F

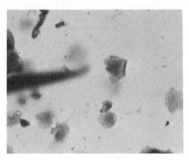

Slide G

approximately four months. Notice the round cells and large nuclei. White blood cells are also present. The next seven slides (G-M) are representative of the estrus cycle of one given bitch. All but the last two slides (L and M) are taken on low magnification (100x) in order to give an over-all view of the smear. The discussion of the slides is as follows:

Slide G   This slide was taken on approximately the third day after the first sign of heat. The cells are under the influence of estrogen and are beginning to cornify. (Note the difference between this slide and slide F) Notice the "trashy" background of cellular debris and the frayed edges of cells. As the season progresses toward optimum breeding time, this "trashy" background will clear up and the edges of the cells will be very sharp and well-defined.

Slide H   This is the smear taken several days after slide G. Notice that the cells are beginning to "cluster." This "clustering" effect is very important and indicates a "healthy" smear. Close examination of this smear under high power magnification will show that the cornified cells still contain nuclei.

Slide I   This smear was taken the day after slide H. The "clustering effect" is continuing and the cells are beginning to become anuclear. Notice that some of the anuclear cells appear almost as perpendicular lines. Notice also that the background is almost clear. Close examination will reveal cells with nuclei.

Slide J   This smear was taken the following day. If one plans to breed more than once, breeding should be done here. Notice the large cluster. I categorically state that even though all the cells in a bitch's smear are anuclear and all other signs are good, the bitch will not conceive unless this "clustering" effect takes place. (However, there is usually an exception to every rule, so breed anyway.) A few nuclei can be seen on the fringes of this cluster, but the vast majority of cells are anuclear. Large clusters do not stain well and may appear almost void of color. A very good smear, but . . .

Slide K   Taken the following day, it is better than J. Notice that practically the entire smear is one cluster, and close examination (slide L) under high power shows that practically all cells are anuclear. This is the height of estrogen effect. BREED HERE!

Slide M   Taken 24 hours later. As you can see, the estrogen effect is over. The round cells with large nuclei and the trashy

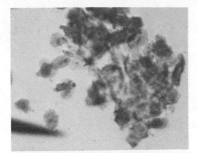

Slide H

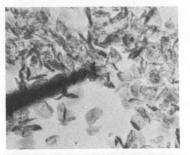

Slide I

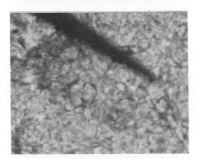

Slide J

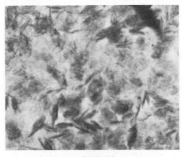

Slide K

Slide L

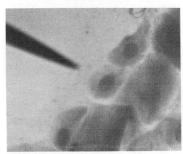

Slide M

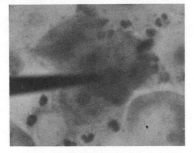

Slide N

background are back. No white blood cells are present in this particular smear, but the noncornified cells indicate the bitch is "out." If the bitch was bred the day before, the breeder hit it right on the nose. (Compare slide M to slide F)

If there is an unusually large number of white blood cells present during proestrus or anytime during the cycle, the bitch probably has an infection even though her smears may look fairly normal during her optimum breeding time. However, when a bitch has an infection neutrophils and intermediate or parabasal type cells often appear at inappropriate times.[4] The clustering effect of anuclear cells does not appear; therefore, success by using vaginal smears is limited if not rendered useless. If such a bitch is bred, more conventional indications of determining when to breed should be used. These include receptivity of the bitch to the stud, spongy vulva or other signs. One other plan is to simply breed the bitch immediately when her smears indicate she is "out." Even though the smears are abnormal during estrous, the smear picture will revert to normal when the bitch goes "out." The bitch will probably not conceive, but the breeding should be tried anyway. I have bred several such bitches in the past three years that conceived. Slide N was taken from a bitch with an infection. Notice that some of the cells are anuclear but abnormally round and notice also the abundance of white blood cells. The bitch developed a discharge a couple of weeks after artificial insemination and was diagnosed as having some type of vaginitis by her owner's vet. She did not conceive.

Notes to the Breeder

1. Learn to do smears yourself. Many veterinarians lack experience in doing smears and most veterinarians do not have the time. Vaginal smears should be done daily for best results. It is impossible to accurately predict what the smear will look like the next day and each bitch is different. I have bred several bitches that had only one day of smears that indicated optimum breeding, and the very next day they were out. You do not know if you have bred correctly until the bitch goes out.

2. Be patient and don't breed too early. It's better to breed late

than early. The object is to breed just before the bitch goes out (before round cells with large nuclei and white blood cells are again noted on a smear). If you should miss optimum breeding time, it is possibly not too late to breed immediately when the bitch goes out, but the bitch might not be receptive. If you plan to breed more than once, breed on consecutive days. Vaginal smears take the guesswork out of breeding. Some bitches seem to go up and down in estrogenic effect, so wait them out, and don't breed too early or you will have to continue breeding.

3.   The purpose of this discussion has been to pinpoint optimum breeding time and to minimize technical language for the breeder. Vaginal smears are no panacea for all our breeding problems, but they do guarantee that the bitch is bred at her best time. The rest is up to her.

Many thanks to Andy Suber, D.V.M. for his continued support and assistance through the years. Also, many thanks to Gary Kightlinger for his advice on microphotography.

References

[1]V. M. Shille, D.V.M. and G. H. Stabenfeldt, D.V.M., Ph.D., "The Estrous Cycle of the Bitch", *Canine Practice* July-August 1974: 34.

[2]*Ibid.* 31.

[3]*Ibid.* 32.

[4]Jeffie Fisher Roszel, "Genital Cytology of the Bitch", *Scope* XIX, No. 1, 1975, 9.

Ch. Mapo's Monica, owned by Mapo Kennels.

Free Whelping

by Rita Little

FOR YEARS there has been much discussion on whether to free whelp or Section a Bulldog bitch. I personally prefer letting the bitch whelp on her own whenever possible. Without getting into the pros and cons of free whelping, here are some hints on free whelping for those who would like to help their bitches whelp naturally.

Always advise your veterinarian when your bitch is expecting a litter, just in case you run into trouble. Some of the complications of whelping should be considered. Though your bitch may be a good whelper, she should never be left unattended, as she may run into trouble.

During the last week of gestation, the bitch's temperature should be checked every six hours. The first indication that a bitch is preparing to whelp is a sudden drop in temperature, usually accompanied by a refusal to eat. Other signs of imminent labor are heavy panting, a swelling and softening of the vulva with a clear, mucoid discharge. Heavy straining motions are the signs of labor. When this occurs the exact time should be noted. Labor can continue for five minutes to several hours before a pup is produced.

First to appear is the water bag. The water bag acts as a buffer cushioning against shock and injury to the pups within the womb and also dilates the passage. Normally, the first whelp should emerge shortly afterward. Nose first, front legs tucked under the chin. With one vigorous contraction the whelp should be expelled, cord and placenta coming away with it.

The newborn pup is encased in a membrane which the bitch will instinctively tear away to allow the pup to breathe. Next she will sever the cord and finally eat the afterbirth. I prefer to tear the membrane myself and cut the cord with sterilized scissors, as the Bulldog's underbite can tear the cord and cause umbilical hernia. After cutting the cord, I take the puppy in my right hand, holding the back of the head with my left hand and swing the pup up to my shoulders and down to my knees, thus expelling any mucous in the throat. Rub the puppy vigorously with a clean towel until it squeals. Then put the pup aside on a warm heating pad, unless the bitch insists that the pup remain with her.

A pup may appear dead upon delivery, particularly on a delayed delivery. Warm slowly and give artificial respiration by opening the pup's mouth, gently depressing the tongue and breathing into it steadily several times. OR immerse the puppy up to the neck in hot—not scalding—water, vigorously rubbing over the heart and lung area. OR put the puppy in the oven or hold it to a warm fire. OR give a drop of brandy on the tongue.

Onset of the next labor should occur within the half hour. Putting a pup to a teat will often trigger the next labor. If a bitch labors longer than two hours, veterinary assistance is needed. After all the puppies have been delivered, and the bitch has eaten at least a couple of the afterbirths, the bitch is fed warm evaporated milk mixed with egg yolk, vitamins, calcium and raw hamburger. The bitch is then cleaned up and taken immediately to the veterinarian for a combiotic shot as well as a shot to contract the uterus to expel any remaining placental matter. It is important to count an afterbirth for each pup and report any not accounted for to your veterinarian.

While the bitch is at the veterinarian's office, the puppies are

Ch. Amber's Trace O'Charger (Ch. Alpine's Mi Amigo Cisco ex Ch. Amber's Delight of Flomar), owned and bred by Doris W. Boyd and Ruth C. Lee. *Francis*

Ch. Charleen's A Li'l Bit of Domino, owned by Mrs. Charles T. Nelson.

being kept warm and given honey water with iron and vitamins by tube. This is given because puppies are born hypoglycemic and hypoanemic as well as hypothermic. I do not put my puppies to the bitch for at least the first four hours. During this period the puppies are fed the honey/water mixture by tube and the prenatal discharges are extracted from the puppies by stimulating the anus with warm, wet cotton balls.

Before the puppies are offered to the bitch, she is given each pup to clean again. I keep my puppies with the bitch at all times after the initial four hours. This necessitates sleeping near the whelping box so I can hear the movement of the bitch during the night. The free whelping bitch is usually very careful not to sit, stand or lie on a puppy. I have found that free whelpers are more careful than Sectioned bitches as they are not under the influences of anesthetics and the puppies seem to be easier to work with as they too have not been exposed to anesthesia.

Possible Complications

Often a breech will occur. Here the hind feet instead of the head are presented first. A bitch will exhaust herself expelling such a whelp and will be unable to pass the remaining pups. If she doesn't expel within a reasonable time, she must be assisted. An assistant holds the bitch's head under his arm, while placing the right hand under and lifting the abdomen with the left hand stretching apart the vulva. The assistant uses a piece of sterilized cotton cloth or a glove for purchase. He then grasps the puppy's foot and with the forefinger of the other hand, enters the vulva and feels for the other foot. At this point both feet should be outside the vulva. The assistant's forefinger is inserted again to wait for the next contraction. When the bitch contracts the whelp is worked out a little further, while a gentle but firm pulling pressure is continued. When the legs are entirely clear, approximately an inch of the whelp's rear can be worked out. Grasp all parts firmly with the right hand and pull in a downward direction, NOT HORIZONTAL, maintaining a firm steady tug. Sometimes it is possible to insert the finger far enough to release the puppy by reaching and pushing from the breast down and at the same time pulling at the feet. If the membrane has been torn off, the whelp's head is exposed. It cannot breathe and will die if not gotten out quickly. Keep in mind, a minimum of time should elapse in getting this breech free. It is better to get the pup away, dead or alive, to save the as yet unborn puppies.

The large puppy which gets stuck halfway can also cause problems. As the bitch strains, work the whelp out. If 15 or 20 minutes pass and you cannot get the whelp out, veterinary assistance is needed.

When the afterbirth does not come with the pup, cut the cord at the point exposed. The routine injection given to contract the uterus will also expel any retained afterbirth.

There is always the possibility of a major complication. Sometimes the veterinarian is not available. When the bitch appears under great stress, insert a finger into the vagina and into the pelvis trying to twist and turn and work the whelp over the brim of the pelvis or perhaps clear whatever obstruction may be present. When doing this, complete sterilization is important. Wash the bitch's hind quarters, dip hands in antiseptic and smear fingers with vaseline or K-Y jelly. I prefer K-Y jelly as it is water soluble.

Other major complications are a head turned sideways. The vet can sometimes turn the head and deliver the pup with forceps. However, it may be necessary to crush this whelp in order to save the others and the bitch.

The whelp presented upside down with the head and rump turned downwards; the back uppermost, and on rare occasions, the backbone lodging across the orifice of the pelvis are conditions requiring forceps and operative measures.

After whelping, keep a close eye on the bitch's milk and her temperature. One post-partum complication that can occur is mastitis. This is an inflamatory condition of the mammary glands caused by milk not being extracted. The bitch usually has fever and refuses to eat. Upon examination, the mammary glands feel hard and lumpy. Apply hot compresses and draw off the milk from the affected teat, keeping the puppies from suckling until the milk returns to normal. Unless necessary, I do not like to give anything other than a combiotic shot to a nursing mother. If after 4 or 5 days the teat does not return to normal, this can signal an abcess, and the need for a veterinarian.

263

Ch. Buster Beauty, owned by Darlene Stuedemann.

Another complication is eclampsia, or milk fever. This condition resembles a fit and must be treated immediately by a veterinarian giving an injection of calcium gluconate into the vein. This is why we feed calcium lactate to all bitches in whelp and continue the dam on calcium lactate while puppies are nursing.

A bitch given good prenatal care and checked regularly by the veterinarian will usually not experience difficulty in whelping. I have heard the argument that in Bulldogs the heads and shoulders are so large the bitch cannot pass them. Aren't we doing something wrong, then? Shouldn't we pay a little more attention to our Standard and keep the Bulldog in proportion? There will always be cases where a bitch needs a Section, but shouldn't this be the exception . . . rather than the rule?

This trio of 11-week-old Bulldog babies was bred and is owned by Mr. and Mrs. Raymond L. Dickens. Puppies such as these are the initiative that keeps the serious breeder questing ever onward toward breed excellence.

265

Ch. Ashford Superb's Brigid, owned by Mrs. A. R. Glass.

Caesarean Sections in Bulldogs

For MANY YEARS breeders and veterinarians have commonly believed that, other than rare exceptions, a Caesarean Section should be routinely performed prior to or at the onset of labor on the Bulldog bitch each time she has a litter of puppies. The rationale for this procedure is listed here:

The Bulldog is peculiar in many respects to other dog breeds and warrants treatment not usually accorded other canines due to its extreme physical characteristics. The Bulldog is probably the most compact dog breed known. The ratio of circumference of the abdomen to the length of the Bulldog is higher than among other breeds. This barrel-shape places more pounds per square inch of internal organs on the floor of the abdomen than in any other breed.

Whelping difficulties stem from two areas in our breed. First, breeders of Bulldogs aim for a large head and broad shoulders and have selectively bred with this aim in mind for the past 60 or 70 years. At the same time little or no attention has been paid to also developing pelvic breadth in our bitches.

267

Some bitches with hormone deficiencies may never go into labor, and there is always the possibility of an edematous pup blocking the uterine tube. Still another hazard that occurs occasionally is a constriction of one of the uterine horns, wide enough for conception to occur, but definitely too small to ever pass a puppy naturally. By the time such conditions are discovered it is usually a high risk case and there is a very good chance of losing a good bitch.

A placid, easy-going disposition is typical of the Bulldog. As a rule they are also often phlegmatic and because of this the muscle tone of many individuals is far from excellent. This soft condition in a bitch is a definite detriment to effective natural whelping. Many bitches can expel one or more pups but can rarely sustain the necessary muscle contractions to adequately empty the uterus. Therefore, a Caesarean section is required. An exhausted bitch with many hours of labor behind her presents the real possibility that her retained pups are not vigorous or even dead. Such a bitch is not as good a surgical risk or efficient mother as a bitch that has not labored long and hard to produce a litter.

One four-year survey of the birth of 160 Bulldog litters reveals only 6% were natural whelpers. A Bulldog bitch was labeled a natural whelper in this survey when she had successfully whelped one entire litter without veterinary assistance. This small percentage seems to indicate the necessity for routine Caesareans in the breed until we correct the relating problems we have bred into our Bulldogs.

There are two different surgical procedures for performing Caesarean Sections in dogs: the flank-type and the mid-ventral type. There are advantages as well as as disadvantages in both procedures.

The flank Caesarean incision is on the lateral aspect of the abdomen and is away from the area where abdominal fluids collect. Thus it tends to be a dryer incision and the wound heals quickly. The Bulldog's excessive visceral weight tends to close a flank incision and it will soon "hair-in."

The flank Section can be accomplished with the bitch on her side, relaxed with a mild tranquilizer (Over-tranquilizing will make the bitch groggy for a day or two and unable to properly attend her pups.) A local anesthetic is also administered, and she remains conscious at all times. Normal respiration and heart beat are monitored and the puppies are born active and unaffected by any anesthetic.

One of the best procedures in any type of Section is the use of an injection of morphine and atropine which does not put the bitch out. The injection of a local anesthetic along the line of incision follows administration of the tranquilizer. In the event the morphine and atropine should begin to wear off, a very mild injection of a good tranquilizer should be administered. Speed is the watch word as in all surgery. If the bitch is overly long on the the operating table the pups will absorb from their mother quantities of the drugs she has been given. If they get large quantities from a long and difficult delivery they tend to cry and whimper for several hours after delivery. This does not seem to injure the pups but will distress the owner who is not aware of the cause.

It is always a good procedure to give the bitch a shot of calcium directly after a Section.

There is less danger of a rupture with the flank incision as this location alleviates localized pressure on the central abdominal wall. There is however the ever-present possibility of a seropurulant pocket forming in a flank section. Also with a flank section there is a greater danger in damaging other vital organs in the bitch. It is also easy for the veterinarian to overlook a pup or two, if the bitch is carrying the pups high in the rib cage, as most Bulldog bitches do. With a flank incision, only one horn is exposed to the incision. The other horn is on the bottom and pressure must be applied to this horn full of pups to remove them. This pressure to the uterus could cause a blood vessel to rupture, a tear or other damage. It takes longer to remove the uterus in the flank Section, therefore the puppies are not removed as quickly. Here again speed is imperative to the well-being of the litter. In a flank incision the veterinarian must go through three layers of muscle not present in the mid-ventral section. However it is not uncommon for a bitch to have four or five flank Sections with good results, alternating from one flank to the other each time.

Some bitches may object to lying on the side which has been incised to nurse their puppies while the area is still tender. A scar may result from the surgery which is cosmetically displeasing if the bitch is to be shown.

With the midline incision, both horns of the uterus present themselves for easy removal from the abdominal cavity. The uterus is completely removed, laid on top of the bitch's abdomen and an incision made in the horns, one at a time. The pups are then removed rapidly and handed to assistants who immediately take

269

Ch. Cherokee's Angus of Primeva, owned by Cody T. Sickle (breeder) and Lee Silva.

Ch. Har Jo's Little Dickens, owned by Dickensbrae Kennels.

the sacks off and begin stimulation, clamp the umbilical cord and clean up the pups.

In making the closure, catgut should never be used as it has proven unsatisfactory; nylon is a much better material. If the veterinarian is careful and sews up each of the three layers of abdominal tissue individually there is very little likelihood of a rupture.

After studying both procedures and making a selection, the question arises when is the proper time to perform a Section. Some breeders have their veterinarians perform the Section 63 days after the bitch is bred. Others begin looking for signs of approaching birth on the 63rd day, the onset of a clear secretion, a drop in body temperature to 100 degrees or less and a general restlessness of the bitch. These signs indicate that the bitch should whelp within 12 to 24 hours.

In either procedure it is wise post-operative care to keep the incision clean and dry. This can be accomplished by simply sponging the area off twice a day with alcohol and applying baby powder or a healing powder such as BFI powder.

In summary, while one vet may prefer one procedure another vet will prefer the other. The doctor should be allowed to pursue the procedure he feels the most comfortable with. If a given vet does not use the procedure you prefer, seek out a vet that uses the other procedure in his practice.

Ch. Polar Princess, owned by Dickensbrae Kennels.

Immersion-Feeding

by Gertrude Freedman

IN searching for more efficient ways in which to do things, we often follow almost torturous procedures when simple ones may be immeasurably superior. Such is the case in the feeding of orphan or undernourished puppies. Most of us have used spoons, doll bottles, syringes with nipples and tubes. We can now consign the aforementioned paraphernalia to the back corner of a drawer, expecting to use it only on rare occasions. Foolish you say. No, not at all, and you will understand why when you read about Freda Samtha, the Kristoffs, and their veterinarian. The story is provocative and puzzling as to why a successful technique advocated by a veterinarian for 40 years, and probably not originated by him, is not commonly prescribed by his coprofessionals.

Freda Samtha was bred to one of our studs and in due time whelped naturally a litter of twelve pups, eleven of which were alive at birth. Four days later a pup died, possibly due to malnutrition, the Kristoffs presumed. Faced with the task of supplementing ten puppies by bottle feeding, Mrs. Kristoff was overwhelmed and she insisted that her husband contact his veterinarian to discuss an easier alternative. Mr. Kristoff, a successful farmer with thousands of head of livestock, automatically called his large-animal veterinarian instead of the doctor who generally treats his dogs and he was told that it was not necessary to use bottles at all. He was advised to prepare a thin gruel of baby cereal and regular milk, to put it in a shallow pan, and to place the puppies in the mixture. The Kristoff's thought the doctor was ridiculous, that the pups might drown, but decided to follow the advice just once. To their amazement, as soon as the pups discovered they were immersed in food, they slurped it with gusto. Freda Samtha, with equal gusto, washed the cereal from the pups when they finished eating.

When I heard that immersion-feeding proved to be very satisfactory on a day-to-day basis, I decided to call the Kristoffs' veterinarian to find out if pups could be fed the same way from birth. The doctor, who wished to remain anonymous, assured me they could. He stated that he prefers the use of a foster mother for orphans, but in the event that none is available, STRONG, PRE-NATALLY WELL-NOURISHED PUPS can be started in the gruel. Right after birth, he explained, they do not lap cereal directly from the pan, but lap each other when removed from the food. In a few days they feed directly on the gruel as did the Kristoffs' pups.

After I wrote my column, but before I had a chance to try immersion-feeding in our kennel, I learned of two satisfactory tests of the method.

Dale Cook (Bulldog Club of Northern California), without any previous knowledge of, or advice on immersion-feeding had tried it with kittens when their dam had died of poisoning. In response to my request for information from anyone who had any, Dale wrote in the *California Bulldogge*, September, 1969, the following:

"I simply used Borden's prepared milk formula, stirring in some pablum, warmed it and plunked five kittens down into it. At first, they licked each other or cleaned their paws. Within days, they were lapping . . . A month later, the vet said they were good, healthy specimens."

Sandra King (Bulldog Club of New England), at my suggestion, tried immersion-feeding on an undersized nine-day-old puppy who was active and strong but ate very poorly. He seemed to find nursing too exhausting for more than very short periods of time, and he did not respond well to syringe feeding. In *The Bulldog Club of New England Bulletin*, September, 1969, Sandra wrote:

Ch. Vardona Hefty Heather (Ch. Hefty Man-O-War ex Webb's Leading Lady), owned by Mary C. Mitchell.

"I placed him in a dinner plate with a half-inch mixture of warm milk and Gerber's Rice Cereal for babies, and after a few moments of surprise and flustered blowing through his nose he arched his neck and began to (eat)! ... It was too deep for him to relax without drowning so he continued to eat until filled and began to cry.

"The next two feedings were not as successful. Once the mix wasn't deep enough ... and once the mix was too thick so that he could not blow it from his nostrils which distressed him. But by his tenth morning ... (he had gained three ounces).

"The fourth feeding was as successful as the first. Later depth didn't matter; the puppy soon learned he was supposed to eat."

In October, in our kennel, I had the opportunity to test immersion-feeding myself. Our Bayside Opal become ill after whelping a litter; one sickness followed another. To relieve Opal of part of her responsibilities I attempted dunking the puppies when they were only several days old. I found that until their dam was so ill that her milk supply was definitely curtailed, the whelps would not take the cereal. As a matter of fact, they crawled out of it, protesting loudly all the time. When the pups became really hungry, they ate so eagerly that I had to remove them from their food for fear they would overeat and become distressed.

Unlike the Kristoffs' Freda Samtha and Sandra King's Jill, Opal, who was really incapacitated by her illness, would not clean her whelps. I bathed the sticky puppies once and put them under a lamp to dry fully, but they trembled with such vigor that I decided to postpone cleaning them thoroughly until they learned to eat from the edge of a dish.

I found that pups did not actually lap their food when very young but slurped it, indicating that the sucking reflex was dominant. The blowing from the nose that Mrs. King described resulted from the enthusiasm with which the pups fed. They simply buried their faces in the gruel as they ate and then literally came up for air, clearing their noses before they inhaled.

In honestly discussing an unfamiliar technique, it is equally important to mention its drawbacks as well as its advantages. As far as I could determine, the only problem that might occur from immersion-feeding is the aspiration of food. Actually as a consequence of aspiration, one of our pups had a runny nose for awhile, but there were no grave results. Of course, a pup can also aspirate milk from his dam or from most types of artificial feeding. Thus, immersion-feeding has no distinctive drawbacks and, except for nursing from their dam, appears to be easier to manage, less time-consuming and nutritionally better than the methods commonly used by most bulldoggers.

Saving Problem Puppies

by Edna Glass

T HIS chapter was written to help the novice breeder. No doubt the experienced breeder has his own methods and his favorite medications to correct the same problems. I would not dispute any other method, and it doesn't matter which antibiotic is used as long as the end result is a live puppy. For years we would lose puppies, always with the same symptoms, and we were always unable to find any solution on our own or through veterinarians.

The following diagnosis and medication comes from an MD who specializes in internal medicine. I will go into detail so the novice will have no difficulty recognizing the trouble in the early stages. The word "early" is most important. After opening a dead puppy for me, the MD diagnosed the trouble as "mechanical pneumonia" which is defined as "a foreign substance in the lungs." This can happen at birth if the puppy is not throughly aspirated, or it can happen later when the puppy is nursing.

The first symptom is a continuous heavy breathing. This is noticeable within a week to ten days after birth, sometimes sooner, but long before the puppy shows distress of any other kind. I compare the heavy breathing to the bellows used for a fireplace. It is not pronounced at first but it becomes more so as the puppy grows and the problem progresses. Do not confuse a slightly heavier breathing immediately after nursing which is only temporary with the continuous heavy breathing associated with mechanical pneumonia. The MD prescribed a five days series of penicillin shots—about ½ cc for a one-pound puppy. Also 1 cc of globulin (one day).

If the trouble is not recognized early, which could happen in spite of every precaution, it will surely become evident when the puppy begins to crawl into a corner, holding its head up, trying to get into an upright position, possibly crying, later screaming, I usually bank the puppy in this position with blankets for it relieves the pressure on the lungs so the puppy can breathe easier. At this point the breathing is much deeper and much heavier and the puppy is truly distressed. Oxygen at a level of two or three liters will relieve the puppy. It is surprising how puppies crawl toward the oxygen to get relief. In advanced cases, the puppy cannot nurse and breathe at the same time, so it is necessary to spoon the milk. I usually add a little baby cereal to the milk. If the puppy turns blue during the feeding, place it under oxygen for a few minutes until it recovers and then continue feeding. Some breeders prefer tube feeding.

Additional shots of Combiotic (Pfizer Laboratories) may be necessary, especially in cases not diagnosed in the early stages. The puppy should be about three weeks of age, for this antibiotic is a combination of penicillin and streptomycin and is *not* recommended at the age of one week. The prescription: ½ cc for a 2½- or 3-pound puppy per day for five days. Also 1 cc globulin (one day). The puppy will continue to breathe heavily long after the shots are finished. Do not be concerned, you have done everything you can, and eventually the heavy breathing will subside.

If you are fortunate to have a veterinarian who will cooperate, he can speed up the recovery by inserting a tube in the lung and drawing out some of the phlegm. This was done to one of my puppies by an MD who happened to stop in to purchase a puppy. I asked a veterinarian to do this for me with a later litter. He refused! Needless to say, anyone who can find a veterinarian who will work with a breeder has an *ace* in the hole!

Again I wish to emphasize, the secret of saving these puppies is early diagnosis, and of equal importance is the nursing care. If you are alert, you can save the work outlined in the last three paragraphs! One more caution, if the puppy appears better in a couple of days, *do not stop the penicillin shots*—continue for the full five-day period. We now save 99% of the puppies with mechanical pneumonia. It is a challenge; it is hard work, but worth the trouble, particularly if later the puppy can add the word "Champion" to its name. This has happened to us.

Another problem we have coped with is digestion. Every now and then one puppy in the litter cannot digest milk. One sign of this is a white bowel movement. If not corrected, the puppy always dies. A pediatrician prescribed Panteric capsules, triple strength, 5 grains, made up by Parke Davis Co. The capsule is too large and the contents impossible to divide for a newborn puppy, so we empty the capsule into a flat dish, moisten a finger and pick up whatever attaches itself to the finger and place into the mouth of the puppy before each feeding. Supplement the puppy's diet as soon as possible with oatmeal and banana baby cereal. The banana supplies the potassium lacking in the puppy's blood which causes the white feces.

A third problem we have worked with is bloat in the newborn—and bloat can kill! There may be several reasons for this but the most common is colic. We recommend burping the puppy after each feeding and giving ½ teaspoon of Digel. It works like a charm. If there is a combination of bloat and diarrhea, we found buttermilk and Digel will do the trick. That is how Champion Ashford Buttermilk Sky and Champion Ashford Buttermilk received their names.

Ch. Cherokee Morgan, owned by Cody T. Sickle.

Tube Feeding Puppies

by Rita Little

O CCASIONALLY, one is confronted with the prospect of feeding or supplementing a new litter of pups either due to the death of the dam or due to an insufficient quantity of milk.

In such cases, I usually rely on tube feeding rather than the time-consuming methods of bottle feeding or using an eye dropper.

Tube feeding has many advantages over older feeding methods. You know excactly the quantity of food each pup is getting. It is less tiring on both the foster mother and the pup. The schedule of feeding is more easily regulated. If overfeeding occurs you can simply withdraw a portion of formula until the puppy is more comfortable. Less air is normally taken in by the puppy, and believe it or not, the probability of aspiration of fluid into the lungs and subsequent foreign body pneumonia is lessened.

For equipment, I prefer using a 15″ Number 8 French infant feeding tube (a clear flexible plastic), suitable formula, a hypodermic syringe—all combined with a small measure of courage.

For the formula, I generally use 1 can of evaporated milk, 1 can of boiled water, 1 egg yolk (dogs cannot break down albumen), 1 tsp. calcium diphosphate, 0.66 cc ABDEC vitamins, 1 tbsp. pure fresh honey or light Karo syrup.

For the first four hours of the puppies' lives I merely work them over every 30 minutes to rid them of urine and fetal residue.

After four hours I try milking the bitch to get some colostrum to provide the puppies the necessary antibodies. If unsuccessful I give each pup about 2 cc. of boiled water with honey.

By the sixth hour I start using the milk formula along with any colostrum that I can obtain from the bitch.

Fill the syringes and stand them up in a cup or jar. Sitting on a comfortable chair, place a towel over your lap. Lay the tube from the pup's mouth along its side and mark on the tube with tape or a non-toxic ink the length from the mouth to the stomach (last rib).

Holding the pup's mouth in your left hand, with your right hand dip the end of the tube in the formula. Lay the end of the tube on top of the pup's tongue and gently slip the tube down the pup's throat.

He should swallow the tube and you should feel no resistance. After the tube is inserted to the mark, attach the syringe. Aspirate the syringe and you should see a little stomach fluid. Slowly discharge the food into the pup's stomach. If when you aspirate the syringe you feel a resistance you are probably against the stomach wall. Don't persist in the aspiration, you might draw blood. As you aspirate the syringe, the resistance, if any, will be immediate. Either remove the tube and begin again or if you are somewhat certain that you are down into the stomach, discharge the food.

After all food is discharged, wait 30-60 seconds before removing the tube to assure that all is okay. Then gently remove the tube from the pup. Wash the tube with warm water, blow clear and begin on the next pup.

Remember: . . . work slowly . . . never hurry! Also, change the mark on the tube as the puppies grow.

In almost every case you will insert the tube in the vicinity of the opening of the stomach or in the stomach itself. If the tube should take another course, the pup will go rigid, gag, and begin turning blue. DON'T PANIC! Gently remove the tube, quiet the pup and begin again. This rarely happens—but it can happen. Feed slowly. As a little test, fill the syringe with either the milk solution or water, attach the tube and discharge the food against your hand . . . do this at different speeds. You will notice as you discharge the food quickly it will sting your hand.

After five days I start putting oatmeal or mixed baby cereal into the formula. By the third week they are eating the formula with either cereal or strained baby food meat in every feeding. By the seventh or eighth day, my feeding schedule is usually 7 a.m., 12 p.m., 6 p.m. and the last feeding at 11 p.m. (This is for mature, healthy puppies only).

Jane Waugh adds: We've used this method for feeding both newborns and for a two-week-old, very sick pup, which was unable to swallow. It works; and it is very effective.

If you aren't sure of yourself after reading this article, ASK YOUR VET TO SHOW YOU HOW IT IS DONE.

We use Esbilac instead of a formula. We add honey and brandy, if needed. And, depending on the pup's age, strained egg yolks (baby food in a jar). We bottle-feed pups that are strong enough to suckle, instead of tube feeding them, but there is nothing better than letting the pups nurse from their dam, if it is at all possible.

Alternate Formulas
One cup milk
One tsp. lactose sugar
One egg yolk
One tsp. lime water
      or
One pint whole milk
One oz. heavy cream
Two tsp. lime water
One egg yolk

Ch. Bayside Molasses Candy, owned by Catherine A. Ganson and bred by Dr. and Mrs. Alfred M. Freedman.

Canine Eye Diseases

by Dr. William G. Magrane

THE sincere, conscientious dog breeder is anxious to learn of any physical condition or disease that might afflict his or her breed. No one is happy to learn of these conditions, but being cognizant of their existence is the first step toward their elimination.

First of all, the terms congenital, hereditary and heritable are often confused and misused. Congenital means existing since birth, or born with the condition. Heredity is the tendency of any living thing to reproduce the characteristics of its ancestors. Heritable means capable of acquiring by inheritance. Environment cannot change hereditary tendencies.

It should be understood that a congenital condition need not be heritable. An abnormal condition or anomaly present at birth does not necessarily mean that it is an inherited defect. The gestation period holds many factors that might influence one or more puppies of a litter. Discussed here are some of the congenital eye conditions which appear to be heritable, but most attention is directed towards the diseases in which there appear to be a particular breed predisposition.

In the normal lid structure of the eye, for man or beast, the lids

Ch. Luthien's Jayjay's Mabel (Ch. Mim-Jim's Buckie-Too of Cha-Ru ex Brookhollow Tinuviel), owned by Jeanne Floro and Mary Frances Gyles (breeder).

Ch. Patterson's Debutante, owned by William and Carol Patterson.

should approximate the globe in proper position. They should not be rolled in or out. Entropion is a condition in which the lid is rolled in. This causes constant irritation to the eye. A simple operation will correct this condition, and unless corrected, there is ulceration and possible loss of the eye.

There is a definite breed predisposition to entropion in Chow Chows, Chesapeake, Golden and Labrador Retrievers, and it has been seen also in the Kerry Blue, St. Bernard, Rottweiler, *Bulldog*, English Springer Spaniel and Bullmastiff. It is more so in some breeds than others, and like other conditions of the eye, incidence varies in relation to breed popularity in a given area.

Ectropion is just the reverse: the lid rolls out, or drops away from the eye. In this you see the so-called "haw" or third eyelid, a very important structure. Ectropion is normal in certain breeds and therein lies some of the trouble. In many cases, breed standards lead to trouble and will continue to do so unless they are changed. There is a breed predisposition to ectropion in the Cocker Spaniel, *Bulldog*, Basset Hound, Bloodhound and St. Bernard. It's easy to understand how the pouch, formed when the lid rolls out, can be a reservoir for dust, weed seeds, etc.

Another condition of the third eyelid is eversion, in which it is curled outward or towards the person examining the eye or inversion curled back towards the eyeball. This condition is seen in the large breeds: the St. Bernard, Bloodhound, Great Dane, Weimaraner and occasionally in the German Shepherd. It usually occurs when the dog is from six months to a year of age. The cartilage is sometimes defective and this cartilage can be successfully removed, the condition corrected, and still retain the integrity of the third eyelid. It is not a difficult procedure to have a normal-appearing and functional third eyelid without the cartilage.

The third eyelid should not be removed except in rare instances, because it is important.

Sometimes the veterinarian is asked to remove the third eyelid because the dog has been "knocked down" in the show ring for lack of pigment. But this is a great mistake. There is nothing functionally wrong with the eye.

People who want the third eyelid removed for cosmetic reasons are gambling on having all sorts of complications. In too many cases there is ulceration, even loss of an eye, because there is no longer a third eyelid present.

287

BIBLIOGRAPHY

ALL OWNERS of pure-bred dogs will benefit themselves and their dogs by enriching their knowledge of breeds and of canine care, training, breeding, psychology and other important aspects of dog management. The following list of books covers further reading recommended by judges, veterinarians, breeders, trainers and other authorities. Books may be obtained at the finer book stores and pet shops, or through Howell Book House Inc., publishers, New York.

Breed Books

AFGHAN HOUND, Complete	Miller & Gilbert
AIREDALE, New Complete	Edwards
AKITA, Complete	Linderman & Funk
ALASKAN MALAMUTE, Complete	Riddle & Seeley
BASSET HOUND, Complete	Braun
BEAGLE, New Complete	Noted Authorities
BLOODHOUND, Complete	Brey & Reed
BORZOI, Complete	Groshans
BOXER, Complete	Denlinger
BRITTANY SPANIEL, Complete	Riddle
BULLDOG, New Complete	Hanes
BULL TERRIER, New Complete	Eberhard
CAIRN TERRIER, Complete	Marvin
CHESAPEAKE BAY RETRIEVER, Complete	Cherry
CHIHUAHUA, Complete	Noted Authorities
COCKER SPANIEL, New	Kraeuchi
COLLIE, New	Official Publication of the Collie Club of America
DACHSHUND, The New	Meistrell
DALMATIAN, The	Treen
DOBERMAN PINSCHER, New	Walker
ENGLISH SETTER, New Complete	Tuck, Howell & Graef
ENGLISH SPRINGER SPANIEL, New	Goodall & Gasow
FOX TERRIER, New Complete	Silvernail
GERMAN SHEPHERD DOG, New Complete	Bennett
GERMAN SHORTHAIRED POINTER, New	Maxwell
GOLDEN RETRIEVER, Complete	Fischer
GREAT DANE, New Complete	Noted Authorities
GREAT DANE, The—Dogdom's Apollo	Draper
GREAT PYRENEES, Complete	Strang & Giffin
IRISH SETTER, New	Thompson
IRISH WOLFHOUND, Complete	Starbuck
KEESHOND, Complete	Peterson
LABRADOR RETRIEVER, Complete	Warwick
LHASA APSO, Complete	Herbel
MINIATURE SCHNAUZER, Complete	Eskrigge
NEWFOUNDLAND, New Complete	Chern
NORWEGIAN ELKHOUND, New Complete	Wallo
OLD ENGLISH SHEEPDOG, Complete	Mandeville
PEKINGESE, Quigley Book of	Quigley
PEMBROKE WELSH CORGI, Complete	Sargent & Harper
POODLE, New Complete	Hopkins & Irick
POODLE CLIPPING AND GROOMING BOOK, Complete	Kalstone
PULI, Complete	Owen
SAMOYED, Complete	Ward
SCHIPPERKE, Official Book of	Root, Martin, Kent
SCOTTISH TERRIER, New Complete	Marvin
SHETLAND SHEEPDOG, The New	Riddle
SHIH TZU, Joy of Owning	Seranne
SHIH TZU, The (English)	Dadds
SIBERIAN HUSKY, Complete	Demidoff
TERRIERS, The Book of All	Marvin
WEST HIGHLAND WHITE TERRIER, Complete	Marvin
WHIPPET, Complete	Pegram
YORKSHIRE TERRIER, Complete	Gordon & Bennett

Breeding

ART OF BREEDING BETTER DOGS, New	Onstott
BREEDING YOUR OWN SHOW DOG	Seranne
HOW TO BREED DOGS	Whitney
HOW PUPPIES ARE BORN	Prine
INHERITANCE OF COAT COLOR IN DOGS	Little

Care and Training

DOG OBEDIENCE, Complete Book of	Saunders
NOVICE, OPEN AND UTILITY COURSES	Saunders
DOG CARE AND TRAINING FOR BOYS AND GIRLS	Saunders
DOG NUTRITION, Collins Guide to	Collins
DOG TRAINING FOR KIDS	Benjamin
DOG TRAINING, Koehler Method of	Koehler
DOG TRAINING, Step by Step Manual	Volhard & Fisher
GO FIND! Training Your Dog to Track	Davis
GUARD DOG TRAINING, Koehler Method of	Koehler
OPEN OBEDIENCE FOR RING, HOME AND FIELD, Koehler Method of	Koehler
STONE GUIDE TO DOG GROOMING FOR ALL BREEDS	Stone
SUCCESSFUL DOG TRAINING, The Pearsall Guide to	Pearsall
TOY DOGS, Kalstone Guide to Grooming All	Kalstone
TRAINING THE RETRIEVER	Kersley
TRAINING YOUR DOG TO WIN OBEDIENCE TITLES	Morsell
TRAIN YOUR OWN GUN DOG, How to	Goodall
UTILITY DOG TRAINING, Koehler Method of	Koehler
VETERINARY HANDBOOK, Dog Owner's Home	Carlson & Giffin

General

CANINE TERMINOLOGY	Spira
COMPLETE DOG BOOK, The	Official Publication of American Kennel Club
DOG IN ACTION, The	Lyon
DOG BEHAVIOR, New Knowledge of	Pfaffenberger
DOG JUDGE'S HANDBOOK	Tietjen
DOG JUDGING, Nicholas Guide to	Nicholas
DOG PEOPLE ARE CRAZY	Riddle
DOG PSYCHOLOGY	Whitney
DOGSTEPS, Illustrated Gait at a Glance	Elliott
DOG TRICKS	Haggerty & Benjamin
ENCYCLOPEDIA OF DOGS, International	Dangerfield, Howell & Riddle
FROM RICHES TO BITCHES	Shattuck
IN STITCHES OVER BITCHES	Shattuck
JUNIOR SHOWMANSHIP HANDBOOK	Brown & Mason
MY TIMES WITH DOGS	Fletcher
OUR PUPPY'S BABY BOOK (blue or pink)	
SUCCESSFUL DOG SHOWING, Forsyth Guide to	Forsyth
TRIM, GROOM AND SHOW YOUR DOG, How to	Saunders
WHY DOES YOUR DOG DO THAT?	Bergman
WILD DOGS in Life and Legend	Riddle
WORLD OF SLED DOGS, From Siberia to Sport Racing	Coppinger